At Issue

Does the Internet Increase Crime?

Other Books in the At Issue Series:

At Issue

Does the Internet Increase Crime?

Stefan Kiesbye, Book Editor

GREENHAVEN PRESS
A part of Gale, Cengage Learning

Marion Carnegie Library
206 S. Market St
Marion, IL 62959

GALE
CENGAGE Learning

Detroit • New York • San Francisco • New Haven, Conn • Waterville, Maine • London

Christine Nasso, *Publisher*
Elizabeth Des Chenes, *Managing Editor*

© 2010 Greenhaven Press, a part of Gale, Cengage Learning.

Gale and Greenhaven Press are registered trademarks used herein under license.

For more information, contact:
Greenhaven Press
27500 Drake Rd.
Farmington Hills, MI 48331-3535
Or you can visit our Internet site at gale.cengage.com

For product information and technology assistance, contact us at

Gale Customer Support, 1-800-877-4253
For permission to use material from this text or product, submit all requests online at www.cengage.com/permissions

Further permissions questions can be e-mailed to permissionrequest@cengage.com

Articles in Greenhaven Press anthologies are often edited for length to meet page requirements. In addition, original titles of these works are changed to clearly present the main thesis and to explicitly indicate the author's opinion. Every effort is made to ensure that Greenhaven Press accurately reflects the original intent of the authors. Every effort has been made to trace the owners of copyrighted material.

Cover Image copyright Illustration Works.

LIBRARY OF CONGRESS CATALOGING-IN-PUBLICATION DATA

Does the internet increase crime? / Stefan Kiesbye, book editor.
    p. cm. -- (At issue)
    Includes bibliographical references and index.
    ISBN 978-0-7377-4878-9 (hardcover) -- ISBN 978-0-7377-4879-6 (pbk.)
    1. Computer crimes. 2. Internet. I. Kiesbye, Stefan.
    HV6773.D637 2010
    364.2'5--dc22
                                                              2010007132

Printed in the United States of America
1 2 3 4 5 6 7 14 13 12 11 10

Contents

Introduction

In October 2009, a man was sentenced to three years in prison in the United Kingdom for committing sex offenses with a girl he met via the Internet. For four months, Mark Talbot, 29, had talked to the girl in a chat room and sent her text messages. She claimed to be 17 years old; only after they met in person in Manchester and had sexual relations did the girl confess that she was only 12 years old. The girl's misrepresentation, however, did not keep the judge from ordering Talbot to register as a sex offender, and the man was also banned from ever working with children. According to the *Yorkshire Post* from October 27, 2009, "Judge Stephen Ashurst said the case highlighted some of the dangers of entering into a 'virtual relationship' over the Internet[,] exchanging intimate and personal details. The judge said it was no defence that the girl had consented to what happened and because of her age, one month short of 13, the oral sex she performed was classified as rape. 'The protection of children from themselves has to be the pre-eminent consideration.'"

Sexual crimes are as old as human society, and it is yet unclear if the Internet has actually increased the number of sex offenses committed in the United States and worldwide. Nevertheless, it seems that every week another case of an Internet-related sex crime makes the headlines. What makes judging the phenomenon harder is the Internet itself, because it spreads news about crimes much faster than any medium before it. It is possible today to have access to news from around the world, and media coverage might give the public the impression—true or not—that sexual predators are on the rise.

What is frightening to parents of young children is that the Internet—easily accessed anywhere via computers and now also via smartphones—is beyond their immediate control. In decades past, sexual predators had to seek out the presence of a child or teenager first, and to risk being seen by friends, teachers, or family members. Yet the Internet makes it possible for children to keep their adult "friends" a secret, and sexual predators are able to arrange meetings far away from home, school, or hangouts.

A good example of the pervasiveness and the danger of the Internet was reported by BBC News on November 24, 2009. Alan Ogilvie, a former Scottish weightlifter and Olympian, admitted "communicating with young men under the age of 16 between 1 September 2008 and 2 June 2009, from an Edinburgh address.... The 41-year-old posted lewd footage of teenage girls on the web, which boys thought came from live webcams they could interact with.... Ogilvie would then record the teenage boys exposing themselves and performing sex acts."

And yet, the portrayal of Internet crimes in the media might give parents and caretakers a very skewed image of the dangers of sexual predators. As researchers Janis Wolak, David Finkelhor, and Kimberly Mitchell write in an article in a 2004 issue of *Journal of Adolescent Health*, the stereotypes about sex offenders are largely inaccurate.

> The prevalent image of Internet sex crimes against minors is of strangers who are pedophiles and who deceive and lure unsuspecting children, frequently over long distances, into situations where they can be forcibly abducted or sexually assaulted. However, [a] nationally representative sample of Internet-initiated cases known to law enforcement suggests a different predominant scenario with different implications for prevention.
>
> First, the offenders in these crimes do not appear to be pedophiles. Pedophilia is a sexual deviation involving sexual attraction to prepubescent children. The victims in these cases were young adolescents. Ninety-nine percent were age 13 to 17, and none were younger than 12.

Second, although they undoubtedly manipulated juveniles in a variety of ways, the offenders in these Internet-initiated crimes did not generally deceive victims about being older adults who were interested in sexual relationships. Victims usually knew this before their first face-to-face encounters with offenders.

Wolak and colleagues also find that with very few exceptions, the offenders did not use force with their victims and did not try to kidnap or abduct them. The teenagers wanted to meet them, knowing that sex would be involved, and many teens met with adults on several occasions after the first encounter. These first encounters usually came about after a long period of frequent communications, and Wolak and her coauthors conclude that it is misleading to call the offenders strangers. They didn't come out of nowhere, but rather had "befriended" their victims weeks or months before meetings.

In short, much of what is believed about Internet crimes has been distorted by the very medium that made these crimes possible, complicating possible prevention strategies. Most campaigns so far have focused on the dangers of deceptive online predators and have warned teenagers not to trust strangers online. Wolak and her coauthors state that

> these may be useful messages to prevent some forms of victimization, [but] they do not address the dynamics of the Internet sexual exploitation found in a majority of actual cases. The data suggest that a major challenge for prevention is the population of young teens who are willing to enter into voluntary sexual relationships with adults whom they meet online. This is a reality that health and prevention educators, law enforcement officials and parents may be reluctant to confront. But effective prevention requires public and private acknowledgment of what actually happens in these cases.

As tough as it may be for parents to acknowledge, their teenagers might have agreed to the crimes committed against them. This circumstance does not acquit sexual predators, as the judge in Mark Talbot's case rightly observed, yet it does indicate the need for a more comprehensive approach to the problem in order for society to keep safe those who are most vulnerable.

The viewpoints in *At Issue: Does the Internet Increase Crime?* explore many facets of Internet-related sexual offenses, as well as cyberbullying, online gambling, and other manifestations of illegal activity conducted with the aid of the Internet.

1

Sex Offenders Prey on Teenagers Online

Bruce Bower

Bruce Bower is a journalist covering science and technology for Science News.

Contrary to common belief, online predators don't target smaller children but 13- to 17-year-olds, with whom they start mostly nonviolent, illegal sexual relations. Even though many parents are concerned about possible negative effects of social networking sites, offenders use mostly e-mail and chat rooms to initiate contact, after which they try to establish an "offline" relationship.

Widespread fears that online sexual predators mainly target naive children are largely inaccurate, according to a new study of Internet-initiated sex crimes.

Instead, the vast majority of online sex offenders are adults who contact vulnerable 13- to 17-year-olds and seduce them into sexual relationships, says a team led by lawyer and sociologist Janis Wolak of the University of New Hampshire in Durham. In other words, Internet sex crimes usually represent cases of statutory rape, involving the exploitation of teens legally defined as too young to consent to sex with adults. Forcible sexual assault and child molestation represent only a small minority of online-initiated sex crimes, the team reports in the February–March *American Psychologist*.

The Public Has Wrong Perceptions

"The things that we hear and fear about Internet sex crimes and the things that actually occur may not be the same," Wolak says.

In 2000, Internet-initiated sex crimes accounted for about 7 percent of reported statutory rapes in the United States, the investigators estimate. That proportion has probably grown since then with increased Internet use and better law-enforcement training regarding Internet crimes, the team notes.

Wolak and her colleagues consulted data gathered via phone interviews in 2000 and 2005 from national samples that totaled 3,000 Internet users, ages 10 to 17. The researchers also conducted 612 interviews with federal, state, and local law-enforcement officials from October 2001 to July 2002. Interviews focused on officials' knowledge of Internet-related sex crimes that targeted children and teens.

Offenders promise victims romance and interpersonal connection but exploit them for sex.

The patterns for how offenders reach the victims suggest that existing educational programs for children and teens may not be effective, the scientists suggest. For instance, they found that teens' use of social networking sites such as MySpace and Facebook did not increase their likelihood of being contacted by a sex offender.

Instead, adult offenders primarily use instant messages, e-mail, and chat rooms to meet and develop intimate relationships with adolescent victims, the scientists say. Offenders promise victims romance and interpersonal connection but exploit them for sex.

Girls Are at Risk

Particularly vulnerable youths often have a background of sexual or physical abuse, depression, delinquency, or serious family problems, Wolak says. They also take various risks, such as talking to unknown people online about sex and seeking pornography on the Internet.

Three-quarters of the victims of sex crimes studied in the new report were girls.

The researchers found that male victims typically described themselves in online communications as gay or as questioning their sexual orientation.

Existing educational programs discourage children from sharing or posting personal information online, warn about deceptive online messages, and urge parents to monitor children's Internet use. Wolak recommends that prevention efforts also teach teens how adults can seduce them into sexual relationships and how to recognize appropriate and inappropriate types of communication from adults.

The new findings fit with evidence that many teens discuss romantic and sexual interests in online chat rooms, remarks psychologist Kaveri Subrahmanyam of California State University, Los Angeles. However, most teens use online forums to extend relationships with friends from daily life, she notes.

"An adolescent not interacting online with offline contacts is a red flag of sorts," Subrahmanyam says.

2

The Danger of Internet Predators Has Been Exaggerated

Larry Magid

Larry Magid is a technology journalist and an Internet safety advocate. He is codirector of ConnectSafely.org and is founder of SafeKids.com. His writing is featured on CNET News, CBSNews .com, the San Jose Mercury News, and the New York Times. He is the coauthor of MySpace Unraveled: A Parent's Guide to Teen Social Networking.

Despite the media attention that online sexual offenders receive, the threat of harm and assault is not as prevalent as feared. Instead, bullying and harassment from peers is a much bigger concern for teens and young adults, and almost half of them experience these pressures online. New technologies, such as age verification, might help cut down on teenagers engaging in adult culture. But to address the true problem, support must be offered to youth who are at risk both online and offline.

A long-awaited report from the Internet Safety Technical Task Force concludes that children and teens are less vulnerable to sexual predation than many have feared. The report also questions the efficacy and necessity of some commonly prescribed remedies designed to protect young people.

The task force was formed as a result of a joint agreement between MySpace and 49 state attorneys general [AGs].

Larry Magid, "Net Threat to Minors Less than Feared," CNET News. January 13, 2009. Reproduced by permission of the author.

Over the past couple of years, several state AGs have been looking into potential dangers to youth, and some have called for social-network sites to use age verification technology to confirm the ages of users in an attempt to prevent adults from . . . interacting online with minors. The task force includes representatives of Internet and social-networking companies, security and identity authentication vendors, and nonprofit advocacy organizations. It's chaired by John Palfrey of Harvard Law School's Berkman Center for Internet and Society. . . .

The overwhelming majority of youth are not in danger of being harmed by an adult predator they meet online.

Based on data analyzed by its Research Advisory Board, the task force concluded that "actual threats that youth may face appear to be different than the threats most people imagine" and that "the image presented by the media of an older male deceiving and preying on a young child does not paint an accurate picture of the nature of the majority of sexual solicitations and Internet-initiated offline encounters."

While the task force found that youth risk from predators is a concern, the overwhelming majority of youth are not in danger of being harmed by an adult predator they meet online. To the extent that young people have received an unwanted online sexual solicitation, data from a 2000 study and a 2006 follow-up from the Crimes Against Children Research Center concludes that "youth identify most sexual solicitors as being other adolescents (48 percent in 2000; 43 percent in 2006) or young adults between the ages of 18 and 21 (20 percent; 30 percent), with few (4 percent; 9 percent) coming from older adults, and the remaining being of unknown age."

What the task force did find is that "bullying and harassment, most often by peers, are the most salient threats that minors face, both online and offline." Partially, because researchers can't agree on a definition of bullying and harassment, the actual risk is hard to quantify, but it is clearly much higher than the risk of being harmed by a predator. Some studies suggest that as many as 49 percent of youth have experienced some type of bullying or harassment. In many cases no serious emotional or physical harm occurred. However, a study by Michelle Ybarra and Janice Wolak found that "39 percent of victims reported emotional distress over being harassed online."

There is also a widespread belief that deception is often involved where adults pose as teens to engage with young people, but research shows that that's rarely the case. The report found that "although identity deception may occur online, it does not appear to play a large role in criminal cases in which adult sex offenders have been arrested for sex crimes in which they met victims online." Interviews with police show that "most victims are underage adolescents who know they are going to meet adults for sexual encounters." This does not imply that such relationships are healthy or safe, nor that we should blame the victims or tolerate the actions of adults who engage in sex with minors. But it does suggest that child safety advocates need to take a more proactive role in helping teens understand the risk of engaging in relationships with adults.

Importantly, the task force found that online risks "are not radically different in nature or scope than the risks minors have long faced offline, and minors who are most at risk in the offline world continue to be most at risk online." For example, "a poor home environment full of conflict and poor parent-child relationships is correlated with a host of online risks."

The attorneys general who called for the task force were anxious for us to study the efficacy of using age verification to help limit inappropriate contact between adults and children online. To help in that job, the task force formed a technical advisory board (TAB) composed of technology experts from

Harvard, MIT, Dartmouth, University of Massachusetts, University of Utah, Rochester Institute of Technology, and Bank of America. This board looked at a wide range of technologies including age verification and identity authentication, filtering and auditing, text analysis, and biometrics.

What the TAB found was that age verification technology can be used to identify adults and therefore help prevent minors from engaging in adult-only activities such as accessing adult content or purchasing alcohol or tobacco. There were several technologies submitted by companies that could identify adults based on accessible records such as credit reports, criminal history, and real estate transactions, but these relatively automated systems cannot reliably identify or verify the age of minors because, as the TAB concluded, "public records of minors range from quite limited to nonexistent." Documentation about young people such as birth certificates, passports, and school records are restricted by federal law for some very good privacy and security reasons.

Age verification options presented by some companies would allow parents to request that their child's school verify his or her identity and age, but these proposals have their own critics, including those who worry about the cost, the possibility of privacy or security leaks, and the financial model presented in some cases that includes providing marketers with information about kids.

The TAB also looked at "peer-based" verification schemes that "allow peers in a community to vote, recommend, or rate whether a person is in an appropriate age group based on relationships and personal knowledge established offline" but worried that with these methods "users can vote as many times as they wish to artificially raise or lower a peer rating." There were concerns that "minors might organize against another minor in their ratings or recommendations in an online form of bullying."

At one task force meeting, a company presented technology that tries to distinguish between an adult and a child by analyzing the bone density of the person's hand. Another tool attempts to identify an individual through facial recognition to match that person against a database of registered sex offenders.

Although the TAB expressed "cautious optimism" about the possibility of using technology to protect kids, it concluded that "every technology has its problems" and that "no single technology reviewed could solve every aspect of online safety for minors, or even one aspect of it one hundred percent of the time." The bottom line was that "technology can play a role but cannot be the sole input to improved safety for minors online" and that "the most effective technology solution is likely to be a combination of technologies."

Using technology to separate kids from grown-ups doesn't address the fact that kids are far more at risk from other kids than from adult predators.

But even if these technologies can be employed effectively, there remains the question of whether they are necessary or helpful. Using technology to separate kids from grown-ups doesn't address the fact that kids are far more at risk from other kids than from adult predators.

Another danger is that age verification or new rules could be used to keep kids off of social networks or require parental consent. But before issuing rules about this, authorities should explore possible unintended consequences such as isolating kids, causing them to go underground, failing to serve kids from dysfunctional families, and preventing kids from accessing vital services such as the Suicide Prevention Hotline or one of the many online self-help groups.

The task force report will have its critics, including possibly some attorneys general and others who feel that it underestimates the risk of online predators. Indeed, sting operations from law enforcement (as well as the TV show *To Catch a Predator*) demonstrate that there are plenty of adults who, if given the chance, would engage in sex with youth they meet online. But, based on the research presented to the task force, it appears that the vast majority of young people are savvy enough to avoid such encounters.

The fact that most kids are safe is reassuring but it's not sufficient.

Still, there remains a minority of youth who—for a variety of psychological and social reasons—are vulnerable both online and offline. More research needs to be done to identify these young people and provide them with resources and protective services. The fact that most kids are safe is reassuring but it's not sufficient. If even one child is in danger, then there is work to be done, and that is one thing everyone who cares about this issue can agree on.

Disclosure: I served as a member of the task force representing ConnectSafely.org, a nonprofit Internet safety organization I co-founded along with Anne Collier. ConnectSafely receives financial support from MySpace, Facebook, Google, Yahoo, and other Internet and social-networking companies. I am also founder of SafeKids.com and am on the board of directors of the National Center for Missing and Exploited Children, which is represented on the task force.

3

Online Sexual Abuse Is a Serious Problem

Michael Scherer

Michael Scherer is Washington correspondent for Salon *and* Time *magazine.*

The case of Justin Berry, a 13-year-old from Bakersfield, California, not only demonstrates how sexual predators use the Internet to contact teenagers and lure them into sexual relationships, but also underlines how the justice system has largely failed to react to the danger of sexual offenders preying on children and young adults. A series of blunders and missteps was exposed by congressional hearings and emphasizes the need to protect children from being targeted and harassed by adults.

Justin Berry, a gangly teenager from Bakersfield, California, succeeded this week in doing what Democrats have failed to accomplish for five years. He persuaded a group of Republicans in Congress to condemn the incompetence and secrecy of the [George W.] Bush administration—in this case, the Justice Department.

"I've got to tell you, my confidence is pretty shaken," said Representative Greg Walden of Oregon during Thursday [April 6, 2006] morning's hearing of the House Oversight and Investigations Subcommittee. Rep. Michael Burgess of Texas announced that he believes criminals are laughing at American law enforcement. Rep. Marsha Blackburn of Tennessee said she found the Justice Department's behavior "incomprehensible."

Michael Scherer, "A Tale of Unsavory Justice," Salon.com, April 7, 2006. This article first appeared in Salon.com, at http://www.salon.com. An online version remains in the Salon archives. Reprinted with permission.

Insufficient Justice

The sharpest condemnation came from the most powerful member of the panel, Joe Barton of Texas, who is chairman of the House Energy and Commerce Committee and a well-known defender of the Bush administration's policies. "We are questioning the judgment of the Justice Department of the United States of America, which seems to think it can thumb its nose at the Congress of the United States," Barton said. "And that will not happen. I am going to tell the attorney general straight."

At the age of 13, Berry had been lured by online sex predators into removing his shirt in front of a Web camera in his bedroom.

As the criticism rained down, Berry, a 19-year-old victim of Internet sex predators, watched quietly from the gallery, dressed in an ill-fitting pinstriped suit. He had first come to Capitol Hill on Tuesday to share his startling and horrifying story.... At the age of 13, Berry had been lured by online sex predators into removing his shirt in front of a Web camera in his bedroom. "The seduction was slow," Berry testified on Tuesday [April 4, 2006], as he sat next to [New York] *Times* reporter Kurt Eichenwald, who had originally told Berry's story. "Each new request went only a bit further than the last."

Before long, Berry was regularly performing online for adult clients who paid him in cash and gifts and met him in person. Some of the predators molested him, he said. One man even rented him an apartment so he could perform for the camera away from his mother's supervision. "My experience is not as isolated as you might hope," Berry told Congress on Tuesday in what can only be described as a heroic act, his voice only occasionally breaking with emotion. "There are hundreds of kids in the United States alone who are right now wrapped up in this horror."

No one knows the full scope of online child exploitation, but authorities unanimously agree that the problem has exploded in the past decade. A recent study found that 20 percent of American minors between the ages of 10 and 17 who used the Internet regularly received a sexual solicitation online within the past year. Experts say that predators frequent popular Web sites like MySpace and Facebook, seeking prey. In one method of coercion, predators encourage the minors to perform sexual acts online in exchange for gifts sent through wish lists on *Amazon.com* or the Web site of American Eagle Outfitters. Other predators use the Internet as a way to arrange meetings with children for molestation.

More than 80 percent of offenders cataloged by the National Center for Missing and Exploited Children were caught with images of children younger than 12 years old.

Predators Are Computer Savvy

In a disturbing twist, just this week the deputy press secretary for the Department of Homeland Security, one of the agencies that testified in the hearings, was accused of an online sex crime. Brian J. Doyle was arrested Tuesday [April 4, 2006] for attempting to seduce a 14-year-old girl over the Internet.

The trade in illegal images of child molestation has also exploded online, experts say. A federal law enforcement task force recently discovered that online peer-to-peer file-sharing systems had been used by more than 1 million U.S.-based Internet protocol addresses over a two-year period to trade movies or images of young children being sexually abused. More than 80 percent of offenders cataloged by the National Center for Missing and Exploited Children were caught with images of children younger than 12 years old. One in five offenders had images of children younger than 3 years old.

The FBI [Federal Bureau of Investigation] and Justice Department have responded by launching new task forces, with Justice increasing its caseload more than fourfold in the past four years. But federal prosecutions still number in the thousands. In one recent child pornography bust, computer records identified 20,000 suspected child sex offenders in America, according to Rep. Bart Stupak of Michigan, the ranking Democrat on the subcommittee. But prosecutors have so far convicted fewer than 2 percent of the suspects. "In Wyoming, our small team has over 250 search warrants we could request if manpower were not an issue," testified Flint Waters, a special agent with the Wyoming Internet Crimes Against Children Task Force.

"Unless something changes, hundreds, or even thousands, of children will be lost forever."

Berry testified about his loss of faith in the ability of law enforcement officials to catch his tormentors. "Based on my case, efforts to prosecute these people are riddled with mistakes and bureaucracy," Berry said on Tuesday. "Unless something changes, hundreds, or even thousands, of children will be lost forever."

Legal Mistakes Harm Victims

After waiting weeks, prosecutors mistakenly released Berry's name in a legal filing, tipping off his victimizers that he was cooperating with authorities. Then the investigation apparently went silent. Nearly seven months after the teenager approached the Justice Department with evidence of his abuse, prosecutors have not taken action against the bulk of his alleged molesters, according to testimony from Eichenwald. Berry's attorney, Stephen Ryan, said the department has not yet taken action on the nearly 1,500 Internet protocol addresses matched with credit card numbers of predators who visited Berry's online performances. Likewise, there has been no action taken against credit card processors that facilitated the business, including one company that is alleged to have repeatedly served the child pornography business.

"I have never seen a case in my experience move slower than this one," said the *Times'* Eichenwald on Tuesday, reflecting on his 20-year career as a crime reporter. "You ask if this is an active investigation. What more can be done? The better question is, what less could be done?"

After hearing Berry's story on Tuesday, members of Congress vowed to take up his case later in the week, when officials from the Justice Department are scheduled to testify. At the time, chairman Barton still counted himself a defender of the Justice Department and its leader, Attorney General Alberto Gonzales. "The attorney general has been very cooperative and we are getting cooperation," Barton said.

But by Thursday [April 6, 2006], Congress experienced firsthand the incompetence that had caused Berry to lose faith. Rather than address concerns authoritatively, the Justice Department refused to send to the hearing any of the officials whom Congress had requested, including those with a supervisory role in Berry's case. Instead, the administration sent William W. Mercer, a pink-faced deputy to a deputy attorney general—a staffer armed with little more than upbeat crime statistics and generic statements of concern. Two other high-ranking child crime officials, one from the Department of Homeland Security and one from the Federal Bureau of Investigation, were not permitted to give their testimony, according to Stupak.

Political Action Is Needed

Both Democrats and Republicans expressed outrage. "We're going to hold another hearing and these people will be here," Barton announced. To prove its point, the panel dismissed Mercer just 15 minutes into his testimony, denying him the privilege of spinning a case that the Justice Department was on the job. As Stupak told an FBI witness later in the day, "You got a very big black eye here on Tuesday, and it is getting bigger every day."

As the members of Congress lambasted the Justice Department in one room of the Rayburn House Office Building, Attorney General Gonzales was giving testimony before the Judiciary Committee two floors down in the same building. Gonzales devoted four paragraphs of his prepared testimony to his "Project Safe Childhood" initiative.

"The Internet must be safe for all Americans, especially children," Gonzales' statement reads.

But as his agency's track record on fighting online predators now stands, such noble sentiments offer little consolation to Justin Berry and other children who continue to be targeted and exploited.

4

Sex Offenders Should Not Be Banned from Using the Internet

Declan McCullagh

Declan McCullagh is a senior correspondent for CBS News' Web site. He became the chief political correspondent for CNET News in 2002, where he remains a frequent contributor. McCullagh writes and speaks frequently about technology, law, and politics.

An Illinois law proposal aims to keep registered sex offenders from using social networking sites to strike up relationships with minors. Yet the broad terms of the bill might make it impossible for convicted offenders to legally use the Internet, which has become a modern necessity and is often needed to perform job searches or job duties. Furthermore, many of the registered sex offenders did not commit any violent crimes and are victims of questionable laws. To protect children as well as civil rights, just laws should address the real dangers of the Internet.

If you believe its sponsors, a new Illinois law will keep sex offenders from recruiting children on the Internet.

"If the predator is supposed to be a registered sex offender, they should keep their Internet distance as well as their physical distance," said sponsor Bill Brady, a Republican state senator, according to the *Chicago Tribune*. "The object is to protect innocent individuals on the Internet from sex offenders."

Declan McCullagh, "Kicking Sex Offenders off the Internet?" CBSNews.com, August 13, 2009. Reproduced by permission.

If that were its effect, this would be a laudable piece of legislation. But in reality, the state law is written so broadly it would effectively prohibit registered sex offenders from using the Internet.

New Laws Might Be Ineffective

It says "social networking websites" are off-limits, and defines those as "an Internet website containing profile web pages of the members of the website that include the names or nicknames of such members," or photographs, or any other personal information. Offenders must "refrain from accessing or using" such Web sites.

Unfortunately, the Illinois state legislature didn't seem to recognize that many popular Web sites—perhaps even the majority of the large ones—fall into those categories.

Google.com features user profiles, including name, photos, and personal information. So do Yahoo.com, Amazon.com, geek site Slashdot.org, and aggregator site Digg.com.

Like it or not, using Google, Yahoo, TV.com, and so on is part of modern life.

Sites like Hulu.com, Netflix, and Pandora do too, as do TV.com, MP3.com, and CNET.com. This overly broad scope makes the law vulnerable to a First Amendment challenge.

(It is surely coincidence that Bill Brady is a candidate for governor of Illinois, whose campaign biography says: "He fought for and passed legislation to protect children from sexual predators.")

Now, perhaps Brady's intent truly was to ban sex offenders from the Internet, although if that's true you wouldn't know it from the former developer and realtor's public statements on the topic. Nor was it probably apparent to his colleagues in the state capitol, where the legislation was unanimously approved by both chambers—or to Gov. Pat Quinn, who signed it into law this week.

Like it or not, using Google, Yahoo, TV.com, and so on is part of modern life, and it's reasonable to hope that even sex offenders could be reintegrated into society rather than cordoned off from it and therefore more likely to relapse. One Justice Department release says that 5.3 percent of male sex offenders were rearrested within three years after their release from state prison.

Brady's legislation also does not distinguish between violent criminals who have served prison time for rape—and adults who are registered sex offenders because of youthful hijinks.

The *Economist* published two stories on this topic last week [in August 2009]. One, called "America's Unjust Sex Laws," says: "Janet Allison was found guilty of being 'party to the crime of child molestation' because she let her 15-year-old daughter have sex with a boyfriend. The young couple later married. But Ms. Allison will spend the rest of her life publicly branded as a sex offender."

Questionable Justice

A second article tells the story of Wendy Whitaker, a 17-year-old high school student in Georgia, who preformed oral sex on a boy in her class. "Her classmate was three weeks shy of his 16th birthday. That made Ms. Whitaker a criminal. She was arrested and charged with sodomy, which in Georgia can refer to oral sex. She met her court-appointed lawyer five minutes before the hearing. He told her to plead guilty. She did not really understand what was going on, so she did as she was told," the magazine reported.

No wonder that a Human Rights Watch report recommends a rethinking of U.S. laws in this area.

It would be one thing if Illinois' new law said "sex offenders shall not use the Internet to harm or seduce a minor," or language to that effect. Unfortunately, the man who would be governor of that state seems to be more interested in taking credit for enacting a law rather than ensuring the right law is enacted.

5

The Internet Might Reduce Violence Against Women

Steve Chapman

Steve Chapman is a columnist and editorial writer for the Chicago Tribune. *His twice-a-week column on national and international affairs appears in some 50 papers across the country. He has appeared on numerous TV and radio news programs, including* The CBS Evening News, NBC Nightly News, The NewsHour with Jim Lehrer, *and National Public Radio's* Fresh Air, Talk of the Nation, *and* On Point.

In the past, pornography has often been seen as degrading and dehumanizing to women, leading men to commit sexually violent acts against them. The rise of the Internet and the proliferation of erotic and adult-content site, and the decline in reported sexual assaults, has invalidated these views, however. The reduction of sexual violence against women may be the result of many factors, but it is safe to say that pornography has done nothing to aggravate this serious issue.

In the 1980s, conservatives and feminists joined to fight a common nemesis: the spread of pornography. Unlike past campaigns to stamp out smut, this one was based not only on morality but also public safety. They argued that hard-core erotica was intolerable because it promoted sexual violence against women.

"Pornography is the theory; rape is the practice," wrote feminist author Robin Morgan. In 1986, a federal commission concurred. Some kinds of pornography, it concluded, are bound to lead to increased sexual violence. Indianapolis passed a law allowing women to sue producers for sexual assaults caused by material depicting women in "positions of servility or submission or display."

As raunch has waxed, rape has waned.

The campaign fizzled when the courts said the ordinance was an unconstitutional form of "thought control." Though the [George W.] Bush administration has put new emphasis on prosecuting obscenity, on the grounds that it fosters violence against women, pornography is more available now than ever.

That's due in substantial part to the rise of the Internet, where the United States alone has a staggering 244 million Web pages featuring erotic fare. One Nielsen survey found that one out of every four users say they visited adult sites in the last month.

So in the last two decades, we have conducted a vast experiment on the social consequences of such material. If the supporters of censorship were right, we should be seeing an unparalleled epidemic of sexual assault. But all the evidence indicates they were wrong. As raunch has waxed, rape has waned.

Crime Is Declining

This is part of a broad decrease in criminal mayhem. Since 1993, violent crime in America has dropped by 58 percent. But the progress in this one realm has been especially dramatic. Rape is down 72 percent and other sexual assaults have fallen by 68 percent. Even in the last two years, when the FBI

[Federal Bureau of Investigation] reported upticks in violent crime, the number of rapes continued to fall.

Nor can the decline be dismissed as the result of underreporting. Many sexual assaults do go unreported, but there is no reason to think there is less reporting today than in the past. In fact given everything that has been done to educate people about the problem and to prosecute offenders, victims are probably more willing to come forward than they used to be.

No one would say the current level of violence against women is acceptable. But the enormous progress in recent years is one of the most gratifying successes imaginable.

How can it be explained? Perhaps the most surprising and controversial account comes from Clemson University economist Todd Kendall, who suggests that adult fare on the Internet may essentially inocculate against sexual assaults.

Both young men and young women are more aware today of the boundaries between consensual and coercive sex.

Controversial Findings

In a paper presented at Stanford Law School last year [in 2006], he reported that after adjusting for other differences, states where Internet access expanded the fastest saw rape decline the most. A 10 percent increase in Internet access, Kendall found, typically meant a 7.3 percent reduction in the number of reported rapes. For other types of crime, he found no correlation with Web use. What this research suggests is that sexual urges play a big role in the incidence of rape—and that pornographic Web sites provide a harmless way for potential predators to satisfy those desires.

That, of course, is only a theory, and the evidence he cites is not conclusive. States that were quicker to adopt the Internet may be different in ways that also serve to prevent rape. It's not hard to think of other explanations why sexual assaults have diminished so rapidly—such as DNA analysis, which has been an invaluable tool in catching and convicting offenders.

Changing social attitudes doubtless have also played a role. Both young men and young women are more aware today of the boundaries between consensual and coercive sex. Kim Gandy, president of the National Organization for Women thinks the credit for progress against rape should go to federal funding under the Violence Against Women Act and to education efforts stressing that "no means no."

But if expanding the availability of hard-core fare doesn't prevent rapes, we can be confident from the experience of recent years that it certainly doesn't cause such crimes. Whether you think porn is a constitutionally protected form of expression or a vile blight that should be eradicated, this discovery should come as very good news.

6

Online Gambling Leads to Crime

Spencer Bachus

Republican Congressman Spencer Bachus holds the leadership position of Ranking Member on the House Financial Services Committee, which deals with such issues as investor protection, the soundness of the banking system, and financial regulation.

The Internet has enabled offshore organizations to offer gambling online 24 hours a day, reaching people in their homes and maximizing the temptation for students and professionals alike. Gambling has always been unlawful, yet the online operations threaten to undermine existing laws. In order to protect families and individuals from great debt, bankruptcy, and financial ruin, Congress needs firm laws banning Internet gambling, while providing the resources to enforce them effectively.

In the history of our country, the federal government has never authorized or sanctioned gambling of any kind. Now, offshore casino interests are leading an unprecedented effort to legalize Internet gambling.

Powerful Temptation

Internet gambling's characteristics are unique: Online players can gamble 24 hours a day, seven days a week from home; children may play without sufficient age verification; and betting with a credit card can undercut a player's perception of the value of cash, leading to addiction, bankruptcy, and crime. Young people are particularly at risk because a computer in the bedroom or dorm room of a young person is a temptation that many may fall prey to.

For more than a decade, Congress has sought to deter, not promote, Internet gambling. It has always been illegal, but until recently no one could enforce the law because the casinos were offshore, far away from the jurisdiction of law enforcement.

The bipartisan passage of the Unlawful Internet Gambling Enforcement Act [UIGEA] in 2006 has helped end this shell game. The federal government was given new tools to enforce old rules prohibiting online gambling contained in statutes like the Wire Act of 1961. The 2006 law was designed to make it impossible to use a bank instrument like a credit card or money transfer or check to settle an illegal online wager.

Even though opponents have delayed and tried to block implementation, UIGEA is already working. According to an Annenberg Public Policy Center survey, after enactment of the law, weekly use of the Internet for gambling among college-age youth fell from 5.8 percent to 1.5 percent from 2006 to 2007. A November 2008 follow-up by the center stated, "The strong drop in weekly use of Internet sites following [its] passage appears to remain in place."

Gambling Can Ruin Lives

Unfortunately, this came too late for Greg Hogan's family in Hudson, Ohio. He described to our Financial Services Committee how his son, the president of his class at Lehigh University, became a gambling addict. Realizing the problem, Hogan installed protective software on his son's computer to prevent him from gambling online. But offshore casinos can find ways to bypass these filters, and the young man accumulated such massive gambling debts that he robbed a bank to try to pay them off. He was sent to prison.

Concerned about the integrity of their games, professional and college sports organizations urged passage of the anti-gambling law. Major League Baseball, the NFL [National Football League], the NBA [National Basketball Association], the NHL [National Hockey League], and the NCAA [National Collegiate Athletic Association], have sent numerous letters to Congress supporting the law, most recently on May 14, 2009. University presidents have shared concerns about the integrity of the athletic competition on their fields and about students betting in their dorm rooms.

Our country has a long tradition of allowing the states to regulate gambling and not permitting the federal government to override decisions made by the states and their citizens. In this particular case, the federal government would be overturning laws in 50 states that regulate gambling. The state attorneys general say they need the antigambling law. Without it, they have no effective way to combat illegal Internet gambling occurring in their jurisdictions.

One company has even developed gambling software for iPhones that will be on the market the day online gambling is legalized by the federal government.

Recognizing the importance of the law, Attorney General Eric Holder promised to vigorously enforce it when asked about it during his Senate confirmation hearing. Aside from the Department of Justice, the State Department has testified, "The Internet gambling operations are, in essence, the functional equivalent of wholly unregulated offshore banks with the bettor accounts serving as bank accounts for account holders who are, in the virtual world, virtually anonymous. For these reasons, Internet gambling operations are vulnerable to be used not only for money laundering but also for criminal activities ranging from terrorist financing to tax evasion."

Supporters of legalization argue that prohibition has sent Internet gambling underground and left the vulnerable unprotected. But it was the 2006 law that finally safeguarded families from predatory intrusion into their homes. The alternatives—age verification and geographic location software—are simply ineffective and easy to elude.

Online Gambling Could Proliferate

Before 2006, offshore Internet casinos were proliferating, raking in more than $6 billion illegally from Americans every year. One can understand why they are spending millions of dollars on lobbyists to try to get back in the game. But if Congress repeals this widely supported law, online casinos will become ubiquitous. One company has even developed gambling software for iPhones that will be on the market the day online gambling is legalized by the federal government.

It took places like Las Vegas and Atlantic City years to develop effective gambling regulations, and they have had decades of experience enforcing them. Yet this new legislation would direct the Treasury Department to set up a new regulatory regime to oversee shadowy foreign gaming enterprises in a mere matter of months.

Even if one concedes that legalization and regulation could possibly prevent underage gambling, compulsive play, cheating by casinos as documented by *60 Minutes* and the *Washington Post*, and money laundering or drug trafficking by criminals on U.S.-sanctioned gambling sites, the pre-2006 problem of predatory, illegal offshore casino bets would return. One country's rules would be woefully insufficient. Ultimately, the results of legalization would be expanding, sanctioning, and inevitably losing control of an industry that offers few advantages to the economy or tax base but incredible pain to families across the country.

It's a gamble that simply is not worth taking.

7

Online Poker Is Not a Crime

Chris "Fox" Wallace

Chris "Fox" Wallace is a professional poker player who blogs for PokerXfactor.com.

Many states, such as Minnesota, are trying to outlaw online gambling, but their arguments about trying to save citizens from ruin are hypocritical, as many states are running their own casino and betting operations. Only if the state cannot cash in on Internet gambling does it oppose online poker. Regardless, a ban on poker, a game that relies on skill, is against American and capitalist principles and would constitute a restriction on citizens' freedom.

On Monday April 29th [2009], The Minnesota Department of Public Safety gave notice to all the major internet service providers in the state of Minnesota that they will be ordered to block service to a list of approximately 200 internet gambling related sites. John Willems, director of the State's Alcohol and Gambling Enforcement Division, says that the ban may expand to "thousands" of sites, depending on compliance. This is not only unconstitutional, illegal, an invasion of privacy and an unecessary limit to our freedoms, but it is profoundly un-American.

I must warn you, I have an inherent bias in this issue. I play online poker for a living. Poker is not just my job, it is my career, and I support my family with it. If this ban is upheld, I would be forced to move to another state. Luckily for

Chris "Fox" Wallace, "Poker Is Not a Crime," PokerXfactor.com, April 30, 2009. Reproduced by permission of Mindwise Media, LLC.

me, every other state in the union would give me a better chance to pursue my career as a professional poker player than Minnesota would.

Limiting Freedom Is Un-American

No other state has gone to this extreme, though Kentucky tried a similar tactic that is failing and was recently struck down by an appeals court. Our neighbors to the north in Canada have not made online poker illegal, [and] in fact they are much more friendly toward online poker players. Can they really be a more free country than we are? Can we really be limiting a freedom that hurts no one, and is not a problem in so many other states and even most other countries? What happened to the land of the free?

The old argument that poker is a game of luck is dead, and anyone who still believes that old saw is thirty years behind the times.

To me, poker has always been the most American of games. In the end it is a game that is completely honest. If I study harder and play better than the player across the table, I make money and he loses. Just like in any business venture, when you succeed, your opponents must fail, and if you are good at your job you get a promotion that someone else does not. This is the very nature of capitalism. The freedom to compete.

Poker does not discriminate in any way. Race, religion, sexual orientation, cultural background, physical appearance, or gender do not matter to the cards; they do not care. You will catch that ace just as often as anyone else, and only your skill, obtained by study and hard work, will determine how well you do. Sure there is short term luck, but in the long run, a skilled player will take home the money, while the recreational player will have more losing nights than winners. . . .

Ask a farmer or a day trader what their results look like, and you can be assured they will be jealous of the consistency of the professional poker player. Even darts champions or professional basketball teams don't have this kind of consistency, and those games are completely skill-based according to the state of Minnesota. The old argument that poker is a game of luck is dead, and anyone who still believes that old saw is thirty years behind the times. In fact, anyone who believes poker is a game of luck is cordially invited to sit down at my table. You are just as likely to beat a pro at the poker tables as you would be to hit a Joe Nathan fastball or beat Kevin Garnett in a game of one-on-one.

A Game of Skill

As defined by the Department of Public Safety's own website, games of skill are not illegal. Here is a direct quote from their page on gambling:

> What about games of skill? If the activity is a game of skill, then criminal penalties don't apply. Skill activities might include darts, bowling and pool tournaments.

So why isn't poker on this list? Why have they singled out my game, the most American of activities, for a prohibition?

The state isn't against poker, just poker that it doesn't make any money from.

Some would say it is because poker has a bad name, and the religious right doesn't want the game played, or perhaps pressure from conservative groups is the problem, but most conservative groups don't support this kind of ban. The vast majority of Americans think they should be free to play poker at their kitchen table or from their computer without the government being involved.

No, when the government suddenly attempts something like this, enforcing a law that doesn't even really exist and trying to prevent us from doing something that is actually perfectly legal, it's always about money or votes. Since this is an unpopular stance that will not help anyone get elected, we have to look for the money.

The money, in this case, comes from the state's officially sanctioned card rooms. In most states where poker is played, Native American casinos offer poker, or independently run casinos are able to offer the game, but in Minnesota, poker can . . . be played [only] at state-owned horse tracks. This means that the money earned from offering poker goes directly into state coffers and they have a vested interest in protecting it. You see, the state isn't against poker, just poker that it doesn't make any money from. And since it can't tax online poker, because the federal government still claims it is illegal to play online, the only thing they can do is prevent people from playing online and force them to play in its state-owned card rooms.

Following the Money

Another quote from John Willems, and again this is the head of the Department of Public Safety, who is spearheading this operation, seems ridiculous once you know that the state runs its own card rooms, offering poker, paramutuel betting [a system in which bets are placed together in a pool], and other casino games, as well as horse racing. From the original article by Paul Walsh in the [Minneapolis] *Star Tribune*:

> He (Willems) did say he has anecdotal evidence that Internet gambling "is fairly large" in Minnesota, noting that Canterbury Park in Shakopee has said that its casino-style games have been hurt. "Also, I've had people call me and say they've lost $20,000; can I help them? I can't."

Apparently the important part here is that those people who have lost $20,000 have lost it online and not to the state's own card rooms. Maybe if they had lost it playing pull tabs or the instant lottery offered here in Minnesota, Mr. Willems wouldn't be so bothered by their loss. If the state gets a piece of the action, then gambling is just fine, and the part about Canterbury Park's casino-style games being hurt points directly at the state intervening to fill its own coffers rather than to protect it's citizens. And let's not forget that the vast majority of those citizens are of the opinion that they don't need any protecting!

Of course Mr. Willems has no interest in whether I am forced to move to Wisconsin because he has made my job impossible for me to do in Minnesota. What does he care about the state taxes I pay when that number is so small compared to the income from a huge card room like Canterbury Park or Running Aces [another horse track card room]? . . . While Canterbury has been successful for many years, Running Aces opened up last year [in 2008] and has yet to make any money. Perhaps the prohibition on online poker would bring more players in and help the state make a profit on their investment? Could a failing card room be to blame for the state making this feeble attempt at prohibition? If Microsoft ever did anything so obvious to try to slay a competitor, you can guarantee that they would be dragged into court immediately.

With millions of online poker players, they can't find one guy to arrest when they claim the activity is a federal crime?

Now we know why the Department of Public Safety is doing this, but will it work?

Prohibition Won't Work

Poker players and tech experts say that there are so many ways around this prohibition that it will not prevent anyone who really wants to play from getting online and playing poker anywhere they want to. The increased hassle would be minimal, and the state has never announced any intention of prosecuting anyone for playing online poker, so there wouldn't even be much of a legal threat. The law that the state is quoting in this action is a federal law, and while the Department of Justice claims that it makes online poker illegal, no one has ever been prosecuted under this law and most legal experts say that it does not cover online poker.

The law we are talking about is the Wire Act of 1961, which was meant to prevent the transmission of sports bets over phone lines. The internet didn't exist, and poker is never mentioned in the law. A number of people, including yours truly, emailed the Department of Justice last year to let them know that we play online poker every day and that they should come and arrest us. We heard nothing back from them. I even included a picture of myself playing online poker, and issued a double dog dare, but received nothing and am still a free man. If they thought this law would hold up in court, do you think they could resist a double dog dare? With millions of online poker players, they can't find one guy to arrest when they claim the activity is a federal crime? I think they know as well as we do that the case would be thrown out of court and then they would have no recourse at all. The threats they use now wouldn't scare anyone and they would have to find another group of Americans to hassle.

Lawyers from the Poker Players Alliance, our lobbying group in Washington, are confident that this ban has no legal basis and will not ever happen, but what if it did? Would I really have to move out of state?

The Ban Is Ineffective

Though I probably would move to another state to avoid the hassle and stop paying state income tax to the state that is trying to prevent me from making a living, I wouldn't actually have to leave. Out of curiousity, I set up a proxy server tonight at home using a free online service. It took about twenty minutes, and I'm not a tech guy by any means. I could probably write a one page tutorial that would allow even the complete tech neophyte to do it themselves in less than an hour, getting them around this ban permanently.

So what do we really have here? A prohibition that is illegal, against the will of the citizens, unenforceable, and that will cost taxpayers' money to put into practice, while effectively doing nothing but forcing a few professional poker players to move to Las Vegas where we should probably be living anyway. Did you know Nevada has no state income tax *and* you can buy beer on Sunday? Talk about the land of the free!

8

Teen "Sexting" Is a Crime

Missy Diaz

Missy Diaz is a reporter for the South Florida Sun-Sentinel.

Unbeknownst to many teenagers and their parents, sexting—the act of sending pornographic pictures via text messaging between mostly high school and college students—is a crime in many states. In Florida, both sender and receiver are held accountable. While some think that charging minors with a felony is overly harsh, parents and teachers should still be aware that sexting is a crime punishable by law and might land teenagers on the list of sex offenders.

At least twice a week, Andy Marun said she saw the same scenario play out at Spanish River High School in Boca Raton: A younger girl sending nude images of herself to an older boy in an attempt to win his attention. And it always played out the same way.

"The boys would usually show the pictures [to their friends] and at lunch the girls would be crying." said Marun, 18, who graduated from Spanish River in May [of 2009].

Sexting Is Unlawful

While teens and parents don't always agree on whether teen sexting—sending sexually explicit images of themselves, or others, via cell phone or computer—is acceptable behavior, most have no idea that it's a crime.

Under Florida law, each image is a felony punishable by up to five years in prison. The charge—typically possession of sexual performance by a child—is intended to snare pedophiles and other sexual predators. But teens who are sexting are caught in a loophole that could have life-changing repercussions.

And here's the kicker: Both the sender and receiver are equally culpable under the law.

Law enforcement in Broward and Palm Beach counties has investigated teens for sexting, though no one has been charged. Miami-Dade [county, Florida] has had no cases reported.

"We investigate sexting like any kind of child pornography case, because that's basically what it is," Broward Sheriff's Office Detective Eric Hendel said. "We get calls when a parent finds material in their child's cell phone and they become inflamed. But they want to back off when they find out their child is just as guilty because they are actively participating in it."

Sexting has exploded onto the teen scene, according to prosecutors at the Palm Beach County State Attorney's Office, so much so that the office is drafting a policy to address it.

"After that Orlando case hitting the papers. I see it coming down the pike," said Lynn Powell, chief of the juvenile division.

Undesirable Repercussions

That Orlando case involved an 18-year-old boy seeking revenge on his former girlfriend, 16, by e-mailing nude photos of her in 2007 to scores of people, including her parents. Charged with sending child pornography, the teen now finds himself on the state sex-offender registry. Last year [2008], an 18-year-old Ohio girl hanged herself after being taunted by classmates after her ex-boyfriend circulated nude photos she had sent him.

Miami-Dade County schools hope to have in place an anti-sexting initiative for third through 12th grades when school opens August 24 [2008], according to student services director Deborah Montilla. The multi-faceted approach includes working with state and local government and law enforcement to review existing laws and training for parents and school staff members.

A study published in December by The National Campaign to Prevent Teen and Unplanned Pregnancy found that 22 percent of teen girls surveyed admit sending nude images of themselves, compared with 18 percent of teen boys.

Accompanied by a detective, Palm Beach County Assistant State Attorney Daliah Weiss speaks to students at middle schools—the age group that seems to be most involved in sexting—to let kids know it's a crime.

"All kids have cell phones and electronic access," she said.

Spanish River principal Susan Atherley already is planning her assembly topics for the coming school year and sexting, along with cyber bullying and the posting of inappropriate photos and content on social networking sites such as Facebook, is high on the list.

"We can't stop them, but we educate them," she said.

After a report from a school resource officer, the Broward Sheriff's Office recently investigated a sexting case at Crystal Lake Middle School in Pompano Beach. Two teen girls sent pictures of a third girl, who had photographed herself in the shower.

"The parents were enraged that this was going on, but when it came down to it, nobody wanted any kind of trouble from the criminal-justice system on their kids—middle schoolers," Hendel said. "I spoke with them and let them know each picture is a third-degree felony if deemed pornographic, and it was right on the border."

Over the past few months, West Palm Beach attorney Guy Fronstin has been retained by the parents of five teens, ages 13 to 16, involved in five separate sexting cases. In one case, a 15-year-old girl sent nude pictures of herself to five boys with messages like "Thinking of you."

Sexting Is Common

Fronstin said he has worked with law enforcement to resolve four of the five cases without charges being filed. A fifth—a 15-year-old boy with numerous images of both acquaintances and strangers—remains under investigation.

"This is an issue that needs to be in a therapist's office, certainly not on probation," he said. "These kids don't even realize it's a crime."

Bill Albert, of The National Campaign to Prevent Teen and Unplanned Pregnancy, says sexting may be the gateway to more risky behavior.

The law should not treat [sexting] the same way we treat Internet predators if this is between two kids acting stupidly.

"In our survey, four out of 10 said exchanging this sexy content in the ether makes dating or hooking up with others much more likely," he said. "Those who exchange sexy content are expected to hook up."

State Senator Dave Aronberg (D-Greenacres) wants to look into carving an exception to the law so that teens aren't tainted for life as a result of a youthful indiscretion such as sexting.

"I hear stories like this all the time, about naked pictures being sent over cell phones," Aronberg said. "To those of us who grew up without cell phones, it's shocking. But the law should not treat it the same way we treat Internet predators if this is between two kids acting stupidly."

Earlier this year, Vermont and Utah amended their laws so that sexting by minors would be charged as a misdemeanor instead of a felony. Several other states are considering following suit.

Albert thinks the key to awareness is parents, who might not even know sexting is on their teen's "menu of options."

Draconian laws or not, Albert cautions that teens are prone to act impulsively.

"It seems a great proportion who have done this describe it as a fun and flirtatious activity," he said. "They also freely recognize there could be negative long-term consequences. What happens here is classic teenage magical thinking. They're aware, but they don't think it will happen to them."

9

"Phishing" Can Fool Even Experts

Tom Regan

Tom Regan is the new media consultant at J-Lab, the Institute for Interactive Journalism, and a columnist for the Christian Science Monitor.

Even Internet-savvy people can be victimized by online scams such as phishing—spam that acts as a message from a legitimate financial organization, the Internal Revenue Service, or a well-known retailer, and asks for personal information. Often, these messages look and sound convincing, and many people submit their social security numbers as well as credit card information and have their identity stolen. Any distracted Internet user might fall prey, and it takes knowledge and vigilance to avoid being defrauded.

A long time ago, my father told me his definition of an "expert."

"An 'x' is an unknown factor," he said. "And a 'spurt' is a drip. Most people who call themselves 'experts' are 'unknown drips.'"

Now, I've been writing this column on personal technology for a long time. I consider myself a bit of an expert on tech topics, particularly on things like computer security and making sure you don't get swindled by Nigerian e-mail scams or phony bank claims. I've issued warnings many times in the past about the need to be on your toes.

Getting Scammed

Then a week ago Saturday [in August 2009], I had a very clear sense of my father's words about experts. I suddenly felt like a drip.

I got phished. Totally and completely. And even worse, the information I gave up wasn't mine—it was my wife's.

Phishing is when criminals send out phony e-mails telling you that there are problems with your bank statement or your credit card account. They are very clever, these phisher folk. Often the e-mail looks exactly like one that you would expect from your financial institutions. There are ways to detect these scams, none of which I put into practice until it was too late. So allow me to go over my blunder step-by-step in the hope that you won't fall victim to a similar scam.

First, I wasn't paying attention. It was early Saturday morning. The kids were buzzing around, the dog hadn't been fed, and the house needed a good tidy. But I stopped for just a moment to check my e-mail. There was a message from one of our credit card companies about a problem with my wife's credit card. Not thinking, I opened it.

Warning bell No. 1: Why would I get an e-mail about a problem with my wife's credit card? If there was a problem, it would have gone to her account, not mine.

Ignoring the Warning Sign

So, I opened it. It said there was a message waiting for my wife on her account. To be honest, at this point, news headlines jumped to mind. "Aha," I thought. "This has to do with the credit card companies upping their rates because of the new credit card rules that will take affect soon. I heard about this."

So I clicked on the link in the message. It took me to a page that had trouble written all over it. But I was still not paying attention.

The page said that in order to get my wife's message, I had to give some information: the last four digits of her social security, password, her mother's maiden name, her mother's date of birth, and other important credit info.

Warning bell No. 2: This actually is not a bell. It's more like the sonic boom that happens when you break the sound barrier. No credit card company or bank will *ever, ever, ever* ask you for this information.

That should have been a gigantic tip-off. But I was still asleep at the wheel. I entered the info and pushed the button and . . . it took me to the regular credit card sign-in page. And that's when I got slapped in the head. "Wait a minute," I thought. "Where's the message?" It hit me all at once. I quickly went back to the original e-mail and clicked on the link again and I looked at the Web address.

D'ohhhh.

My stupidity cost me $20 a month for me and my wife to protect ourselves.

Checking the Web Address

It was a phony. One of the best ways to tell if you are being scammed is to look at the Web address. A real bank or credit card company's address is pretty straightforward: like www .citibank.com, for instance. But a phony Web address will be something like www.hel.ge.citibank.ge. There are *always* extra letters or numbers. If you're not sure, just call and ask if it's real.

I immediately called my wife's credit card company and told them we had been phished. They canceled her card on the spot and we changed the password to get into the account. I also signed up with one of the identity theft protection companies, which immediately sent out a warning to all concerned credit card companies to keep an eye out for strange activity. My stupidity cost me $20 a month for me and my wife to protect ourselves. It's not a big cost, but it's a bit like closing the barn door after the horse is already out.

So be vigilant. These folks are extremely tricky. They count on people being distracted to do something dumb like I did.

You don't have to be an "unknown drip" to get caught on the end of a phishing hook.

10

E-mail Reform Is Necessary to Prevent "Phishing"

PR Newswire

PR Newswire delivers news and multimedia content to investors, media, and consumers.

Phishing and Internet scams have led to many problems, including identity theft. The National Consumers League (NCL) has called for action to combat this growing problem. The NCL recommends consumer education, better tools for investigation, and ways to authenticate e-mail users as ways to fight against phishing. It is only a widespread adoption of these ideas that will halt the scams.

Consumer confidence in conducting business and protecting personal data online is threatened every day by phishing scams. In an initiative led by the National Consumers League (NCL), law enforcement, financial services and technical industries have joined forces to combat this threat. The group today issued a "call to action" with the release of a paper outlining key recommendations that form a comprehensive plan for combating phishing more effectively.

Phishing is a large and growing problem, in which identity thieves pose as legitimate companies, government agencies, or other trusted entities in order to trick consumers into providing their bank account numbers, Social Security numbers, and other personal information. In 2005, phishing scams ranked

PR Newswire, "Groups Unite to Issue 'Call for Action' Against Phishing Scams," March 16, 2006.

6th in Internet complaints to NCL's Internet Fraud Watch program, and the scams continue to dupe consumers. A May 2005 consumer survey by First Data found that 43 percent of respondents had received a phishing contact, and of those, 5 percent (approximately 4.5 million people) provided the requested personal information. Nearly half of the phishing victims, 45 percent, reported that their information was used to make an unauthorized transaction, open an account, or commit another type of identity theft.

"We all need to work together if we want to have a significant impact on the tidal wave of phishing."

How to Combat Phishing

NCL's new report, the result of a comprehensive three-day brainstorming retreat organized by the Washington-based consumer advocacy organization last September, makes multiple recommendations on how to combat it.

"There is no silver bullet to solve the phishing problem, but there are known responses that need more support and promising new approaches that could help deter it," said Susan Grant, director of NCL's National Fraud Information Center. The key recommendations in the report are:

- Create systems that are "secure by design" to make consumers safer online without having to be computer experts;

- Implement better ways to authenticate email users and Web sites to make it easier to tell the difference between legitimate individuals and organizations and phishers posing as them;

- Provide better tools for investigation and enforcement to prevent phishers from taking advantage of technology, physical location, and information-sharing barriers to avoid detection and prosecution;

- Learn from the "lifecycle of the phisher" and use that knowledge about how these criminals operate to exploit points of vulnerability and stop them;

- Explore the use of "white lists" to identify Web sites that are spoofing legitimate organizations and use "black lists" to create a phishing recall system that would prevent phishing messages from reaching consumers;

- Provide greater support for consumer education, using clear, consistent messages and innovative methods to convey them.

We all need to work together if we want to have a significant impact on the tidal wave of phishing.

Sponsorship for the initiative was provided by the American Express Company, First Data Corporation, and Microsoft Corporation. The recommendations were developed by retreat participants representing financial services firms, Internet service providers, online retailers, computer security firms, software companies, consumer protection agencies, law enforcement agencies, consumer and ID theft victim organizations, academia, and coalitions such as the Anti-Phishing Working Group and the National Cyber Security Alliance. Peter Swire, C. William O'Neill Professor of Law at the Moritz College of Law of the Ohio State University, wrote the report for NCL.

In the next phase of this project, NCL is forming working groups and inviting organizations and experts who are concerned about phishing to examine how the anti-phishing strategies in the report can be adopted on a widespread basis. "We all need to work together in a systematic approach if we want to have a significant impact on the tidal wave of phishing that is hitting consumers and hurting legitimate organizations," said Grant.

11

Cyberbullying Is a Menace to Educators

Mary Bousted

Mary Bousted is the general secretary of the Association of Teachers and Lecturers in Great Britain.

Whereas schoolyard bullies usually pick on weaker or younger children, cyberbullies attack an increasing number of teachers and professors by disseminating vicious rumors, sending online threats, or posting offensive content on Web sites. Schools and colleges need to combat this trend if they want to keep students, teachers, and staff safe. Bullying needs to be punished swiftly, and harmful content needs to be spotted and removed quickly and efficiently to make the Internet safe for its users.

Cyber-bullying is a menace—and a growing menace. But unlike most other forms of bullying it can be done virtually anonymously and from afar—using phones, email and the internet. And the bullying can be spread and circulated endlessly before the victim is aware of what has happened.

Victims don't have to be weaker than the bully, or outnumbered. Victims can be children. But increasingly they are adults.

While the government's guidance, issued on 21 September [2007] should help schools tackle cyber-bullying of pupils, it fell short of completely addressing the needs of adult victims.

Mary Bousted, "Tackling the Threat of Cyber Bullying," publicservice.co.uk, October 1, 2007. Reproduced by permission.

And increasingly those working in education—catering staff, librarians, teaching assistants, teachers, and even deputies and heads—are falling victim.

ATL [Association of Teachers and Lecturers] is getting contacted by a rising number of members who have had offensive comments or images of them posted on websites such as YouTube and Facebook. In a survey this year [2007], 17 per cent of members said they have been victims of cyber-bullying. Many have been distressed and humiliated. And unsurprisingly, considering the nature of the bullying. Some teachers have received online rape and death threats, and others have had a photo of them projected onto pornographic pictures.

Cyber-Bullies Prove Evasive

If this type of bullying took place face to face we would expect the perpetrators to be prosecuted and sentenced for breaking the law. Yet with cyber-bullying this proves incredibly difficult and in many cases impossible because the bully is anonymous, or overseas so not subject to UK [United Kingdom] law, or the website is based overseas and is not subject to UK law.

So what can be done to combat cyber-bullying of school and college staff?

Schools and colleges should recognise that cyber-bullying is a health and safety issue.

We want website hosts to take firmer action to block offensive material. This April [in 2007], while he was Education Secretary, Alan Johnson supported our call for website hosts to be more responsible for what is posted on their websites.

We think it is unacceptable that offensive material can appear on a website for several weeks or months before it comes to the attention of the victim. The hosts should be more vigilant when monitoring the appropriateness of student comments and video clips, and prevent offensive material being posted. They should also be required to incorporate easily accessible complaints procedures into their website so that people can register their concerns.

Schools and colleges also have a role to play themselves. They should incorporate measures to combat cyber-bullying of staff into their anti-bullying policies. And they should discipline any students who have submitted offensive material to a website.

Schools and colleges should recognise that cyber-bullying is a health and safety issue, which means they have a duty of care towards the well-being of any staff who are cyber-bullied. As the employer, the school, college or local authority should contact the website hosts and insist that any offensive material is removed within 24 hours. And if the material is deemed threatening and/or intimidating, the employer should, with the victim's consent, report the issue to the police.

The Government Must Step In

We also want government ministers to take a lead on this crucial issue. We believe there is a strong case for introducing an independent ombudsman to investigate complaints of cyber-bullying. And we would like the Government to treat bullying of those working in education as seriously as it does cyber-bullying of children. . . .

We don't want to be killjoys demanding schools block access to websites and phones. Rather we want to send a message that bullying, in all its forms whether in school or on the web, is totally unacceptable and will not be tolerated. That regardless of the age of the victim, bullying will be tackled firmly and the bullies punished. That passing [along] false or offensive material about someone is also a form of bullying. And to make everyone understand that standing, or sitting by, while someone is bullied makes the bystander a colluder in the bullying.

Everyone at school deserves to be treated with respect—pupils and staff alike. If we are all to continue enjoying using mobiles and the internet we need to be vigilant to ensure users behave responsibly, anything offensive is removed fast, and bullies are dealt with appropriately.

12

Cyberbullying Should Not Be Dealt with in Courts

Emily Bazelon

Emily Bazelon is a Slate *senior editor and an editor of* DoubleX *magazine. Her work focuses primarily on the justice system and family issues.*

When Lori Drew, a suburban mother, created the fake profile of 16-year-old "Josh" to harass Megan Meier, a former friend of her teenage daughter, she became an infamous example of a cyberbully. Meier killed herself after an especially nasty message from "Josh," but the court rightfully did not convict Drew of any felonies. Free speech needs to be protected from overeager lawmakers and judges who want to restrict Internet use for safety purposes. And even though incidents such as the Lori Drew case are regrettable, they do not necessitate censorship. Meier's death is about families and neighborhood relationships, not about cutting down the First Amendment.

As a matter of law, the verdict against Lori Drew in the MySpace suicide case is fairly indefensible. A U.S. attorney in Los Angeles went after a misdeed in Missouri—when state and federal prosecutors there didn't think Drew's actions constituted a crime—with a crazy-broad reading of a statute written to punish computer hacking. Just about every single law professor and editorial writer to weigh in has condemned the prosecutorial overreaching. But the failure to make a valid case against Drew begs a larger question: Is there a better way to go after cyber-bullying? Or is this the kind of troublemaking, however nefarious, the government shouldn't try to punish?

Megan hanged herself in her bedroom.

Cyber-Bullying Ends in Tragedy

Drew is the mother from hell who famously tried to defend her own teenage daughter against rumor-mongering on the Internet by creating the MySpace persona of fictional 16-year-old Josh Evans, then using that persona to fire off personal e-mail attacks (or sometimes spurring a young women she worked with to do that). Twenty minutes after "Josh" sent 13-year-old Megan Meier, Drew's daughter's erstwhile friend, the message "the world would be a better place without you," Megan hanged herself in her bedroom.

Someone other than Drew apparently sent that last dreadful e-mail. Even if she had, it seems wrong to say she caused Megan's death. We're talking about an adolescent who must have been vulnerable and volatile and who was taking antidepressants. But the local sheriff's department's dismissal of Drew's MySpace foray as merely "rude" and "immature" doesn't seem proportionate, either. Drew was an adult who secretly entered a teenage world and made it more dangerous. A girl in that world died. The formulation that makes sense to me is that Drew at least contributed to Megan's suicide. So did the abstract verbal brutality of e-mail and the humiliation and shunning made possible by MySpace. But the vacuum cleaner that would cleanse the Web of its pseudonymous nastiness would also suck up a lot of free speech. Freedom often doesn't go with niceness.

The problems with the California case against Drew started with the poor fit between her wrongdoing and the law used to punish her. The federal Computer Fraud and Abuse Act [CFAA] makes it a crime to intentionally access "a computer without authorization." So what does that mean—is it a crime to hack past a password or a firewall? Or merely to violate a terms-of-service contract like the one MySpace users agree to?

> The federal Computer Fraud and Abuse Act makes it a crime to intentionally access "a computer without authorization."

In 2003, George Washington University law professor Orin Kerr wrote a prescient law-review article arguing for the former, narrower interpretation. The legislative history for the CFAA indicates that Congress wasn't trying to prosecute any or every breach of contract. Would lawmakers really want to go after people, even potentially, for giving a fake name to register for a Web site, for example (dressed up as the bad act of giving "false and misleading information")? Nor, for that matter, does it look as if Congress intended to base prison time on the MySpace contractual provision that bars use of the site that "harasses or advocates harassment of another person" or that is "abusive, threatening, obscene, defamatory, or libelous." It's one thing for MySpace to kick someone out for acting like a troll or even for the troll's target to sue her. It's another thing entirely to throw the weight of the government behind a criminal investigation and conviction for what usually just amounts to mischief in cyber-contracts.

No Legal Case

In the Lori Drew prosecution, the theory was that Drew was on the hook for setting up the fake profile, then using it to inflict emotional distress. Three of the four counts against Drew were for "unauthorized access" of MySpace simply because

Drew violated the MySpace terms of service to which she agreed, according to Los Angeles U.S. Attorney Thomas O'Brien's dubious interpretation. The jury didn't think the prosecutors proved the emotional distress and so dismissed the fourth count. And they knocked down the other charges from felonies to misdemeanors. But they did buy the idea that Drew "intentionally" broke the law, even though all that seems to mean is that she clicked "I agree" in response to a long series of legalistic paragraphs that just about nobody really reads. It's hard to imagine even these misdemeanor convictions standing up on appeal.

Kerr joined Drew's defense team, and his post last Friday [in late 2008] on the Volokh Conspiracy blog gets at just how ludicrous it is to imagine every breach of a Web site's terms of service as a federal crime. (Kerr: By visiting the Volokh Conspiracy, you agree that your middle name is not Ralph and that you're "super nice." You lied? Gotcha.) Of course, prosecutors aren't really going to investigate all the criminals Kerr just created with the terms of service in his post. But this is not a road we want to take even one baby step down. As Andrew Grossman argues for the Heritage Foundation, laws that make it seem as if "everyone is a criminal" are generally a bad idea. Most of the time, they're unenforceable, and then every once in a while, they're used to scapegoat someone like Lori Drew.

What about a law written expressly to address cyberbullying? Such a statute could presumably direct prosecutors to go after only the worst of the Internet meanies. Or, then again, maybe not. A proposed bill before Congress is far broader. It targets anyone who uses "electronic means" to transmit "in interstate or foreign commerce any communication, with the intent to coerce, intimidate, harass, or cause substantial emotional distress to a person." The penalty is a fine or imprisonment for up to two years.

Missouri, where Meier lived, has already passed a cyber-bullying law. The Missouri statute extends the state's bar on phone harassment to computers. The problem with the analogy is that the computer context is more dangerous to free speech: On the phone, you talk to one other person. On My-Space or any other Web site, you broadcast to as many people as read you. Other states have passed laws giving schools more authority to address cyber-bullying. That sounds better, but it could get schools too involved in disciplining students for the IMs [instant messages] and posts they write from home.

The Internet doesn't really call for rethinking our affection for the First Amendment.

All of this takes us back to earlier battles over prosecuting hate speech. As Eugene Volokh points out on his ever-vigilant blog, the cyber-bullying bill before Congress is a classic example of a law that's unconstitutional because it's overly broad. The Supreme Court has held that the First Amendment protects "outrageous" speech—from civil as well as criminal liability—even if it "recklessly, knowingly, or purposefully causes 'severe emotional distress,' when it's about a public figure." Volokh adds, "Many, though not all, lower courts have held the same whenever the statement is on a matter of public concern, even about a private figure."

That doesn't mean that a cyber-bullying statute as applied to a Lori Drew-like horror show would be unconstitutional; "Josh's" trashing of Megan was hardly a matter of public concern. But even if a better drafter could come up with a narrower law, since when do we want the government to go after bullies when the only weapon they wield is words? Other countries have experimented with prosecuting hate speech; they don't think their civil traditions are strong enough to withstand, for example, ethnically based calls to violence. But that's not a direction American law has ever taken. And wild and woolly though it may be, the Internet doesn't really call for rethinking our affection for the First Amendment. Cyber-bullying is scary. For some kids, MySpace isn't a safe place. But criminal convictions aren't the best way to clean up the neighborhood.

13

Developing Countries Pose a Safety Risk to Western Internet Users

Richard Bowman

Richard Bowman is regional manager of MessageLabs South Asia, a web and e-mail security firm. Based in Singapore, he is responsible for all aspects of business development in South Asia.

With increased computer activity in developing nations where Internet security is very low, viruses, botnets, and spam have also increased manifold and are threatening relatively secure systems worldwide. Companies, corporations, and governments spend billions every year to counteract waves of online crime and spam, and while spam and phishing will be hard to eradicate, online users should invest in managed security services that can detect the viruses and malware conventional anti-virus software fails to detect.

The rise of an Internet-savvy middle class in developing countries such as India and China has created a fertile launching pad for the distribution of viruses, spam and malware, which the 'bad guys' are now using. As India and China come online through their middle class, it introduces new security challenges for the broader Western world.

On the Internet, everything is connected to everything else. Distance does not separate a business in London from a virus-compromised home computer in Bangalore or Beijing.

Richard Bowman, "Developing World, Developing Problems," *MIS Asia Magazine*, April 24, 2009. Copyright © 2009, Fairfax Media. Reproduced by permission.

The problem for businesses anywhere in the world is that the more compromised computers there are, the greater the torrent of malware and spam.

India and China are in the news because of their tremendous economic growth. The Chinese economy expanded by 9.8 per cent in 2008 and the Indian economy by 6.6 per cent.

The Dangers of Broadband

This economic power is matched by a growing number of Internet-connected computers and a growing middle class with broadband access at home. India had 81 million Internet users in 2008, while China had 298 million in 2008.

Where we see increased virus activity in a region, botnets and spam follow.

In our experience, it is not just the number of computers or Internet users that cause problems for our customers, but the number of broadband connections. Why? First, when a computer is permanently connected to the Internet, it is easier to infect with a virus. Second, an infected computer can join a botnet and start spamming other Internet users or sending out more viruses. Worse, it can do it at a high speed, 24 hours a day.

Broadband statistics show relentless growth for the developing economies. By the end of 2008, the Asia-Pacific region had more than 171 million broadband subscribers—an increase of 31.5 per cent over the previous year.

Where we see increased virus activity in a region, botnets and spam follow. Our hypothesis is that users in developing countries may be new to the Internet and unaware of the risks they run when they go online and the techniques they need to apply in order to protect themselves.

In 2008, spammers developed an affinity for spamming from large, reputable Web-based e-mail and application services by defeating CAPTCHA (completely automated public Turing test to tell computers and humans apart) techniques to generate massive numbers of personal accounts from these services. Complex Web-based malware targeting social networking sites and vulnerabilities in legitimate Web sites also became widespread in 2008, resulting in malware being installed onto computers with no user intervention required.

Malware Attacks Are on the Rise

Other methods of malware attack common in 2008 also included attacks disguised as free application downloads and games targeted at new smart phones, and targeted trojan attacks that rose to a peak of 98 per day in December 2008. Towards the end of 2008, the credit crisis generated many new finance-related attacks as spammers and scammers sought to take advantage of the panic and uncertainty.

In 2009, phishing attacks will focus on exploiting vulnerable DNS [domain name system] domains and Web sites while any Web site that requires a personal account to be created online will continue to be targeted and the CAPTCHA failure rate will continue to increase accordingly. MessageLabs [an Internet security firm] experts also predict that in 2009 the emerging markets will be more heavily targeted with spam delivered in the local language.

Growth in foreign language spam, especially Asian character spam, will increase by 100 per cent from current levels (five per cent) to around 10 per cent. In 2009, the major botnets disrupted by the takedown of Intercage [an Internet service provider] and McColo [a Web hosting company] at the end of 2008 are expected to find replacement hosting services in countries such as Russia, Brazil or China. . . .

When we publish data that say that developing economies are the source of a lot of spam, people get concerned because they think there is hacker activity there. That is a concern, but the bigger threat is the rise of consumer IT [information technology] and the lack of protection of it. If you get some new green fields on the Internet, there's a period when security is lax and viruses run wild. The situation is similar to the one we faced here a few years ago. However, the big difference is that exploits are much more sophisticated today, so an unprotected PC [personal computer] is much more vulnerable.

The Threat Landscape

MessageLabs secures 2.5 billion e-mail connections and 1.5 billion Web requests every day. This gives us valuable insight into the dangers lurking on the Internet. Overall, spam levels have remained stable, but high, for the last year. In March 2009 alone, 75.7 per cent of all the e-mails we scanned globally contained spam. This increase may possibly correlate to new botnets emerging in green field Internet sites such as India and China. . . .

Online criminal activity is worth billions.

There are some worrying trends that show that Internet criminals are upping their game. First, they are increasingly sending links to malicious websites that install malware rather than including malware in the e-mail itself. Some botnets also hide the true location of spam, malware and phishing sites behind rapidly-changing addresses of Web proxies for each domain. This technique accounted for the increase of botnets from 20 per cent to 25 per cent by mid-2008. In addition, the botnets that they create are much more resilient. It is increasingly difficult to detect, disrupt or remove them.

These moves make it harder for conventional defences to protect computers. They also make it more important than ever to block these attacks before they reach the user. An ounce of prevention is worth a pound of cure.

The Shadow Economy and Targeted Attacks

Online criminal activity is worth billions. There is a sophisticated shadow economy online with tens of thousands of participants where technical experts collaborate with criminal gangs to make money. There are specialist malware writers, botnet owners, identity thieves, spammers and a shady network of middlemen and market makers. It has all the attributes of the real world economy—division of labour, price competition, marketing, even guarantees.

Just as large corporations are eager to open up new markets in the developing world, so do online criminals see a burgeoning and relatively unprotected pool of Internet users as a huge opportunity.

From late 2008 to 2009, the U.S. Pentagon spent more than US$100 million clearing up Internet attacks and viruses.

Another sign of growing sophistication in the shadow economy is the continuous improvement in product quality. Malware writers work hard to test their products against anti-virus software. They offer guarantees that a given virus or trojan will not be detected using conventional anti-virus programs. If vendors update their software, then the malware author will supply a new version. Unfortunately for them, they cannot buy a copy of MessageLabs or other managed security services so they cannot guarantee against these services.

According to industry experts, the shadow Internet economy was worth more than US$105 billion in 2008. 2009 is predicted to be another year of significant growth as e-crime tools become accessible and the market becomes more mature and open, operating to conventional supply and demand rules. Through the continuous improvement in the quality of products on sale in the shadow economy, previous barriers to entry such as technical skills will be lowered and more people will try and make a living out of this economy.

Prevention Is Better than Cure

It is easy to dismiss Internet problems as 'out there,' 'too techie to deal with' and 'not my problem,' especially by smaller businesses that may not have dedicated IT staff. The reality is that Internet crime hurts businesses. In 2008, the US authorities indicted a spammer who ripped off US$3 million through a stock spam scam. From late 2008 to 2009, the US Pentagon spent more than US$100 million clearing up Internet attacks and viruses. The most common form of attack is via e-mail or a rogue website. In addition, 70 per cent of all e-mail traffic is unwanted spam, a waste of time and server capacity.

Protecting confidential data is a growing concern for businesses. Not only must they comply with regulations, including the Data Protection Act, but [they must] also deal with security breaches, which can have a serious impact on a company's reputation and share price. This is why the latest form of attack, the targeted trojan, is a real concern. Specifically written and designed for information theft, attackers use public information, such as Companies House [a UK foundation that gathers puclic information about businesses] records or information from social networking sites, to target key individuals by name.

Because [such] malware is a one-off [unique], conventional anti-virus software, which uses signatures to spot viruses, has a hard time detecting it. Moreover, as it is carefully targeted at individuals, it has a greater chance of getting through. In 2005, we saw about two such attacks a week—and this figure increased to two attacks a day in 2006. By 2008, this figure increased exponentially to an average of 53 such attacks per day globally.

Be Certain in an Uncertain World

A looming virus and spam threat from developing countries, combined with the rise of new forms of malware and targeted trojans, makes the threat landscape a very populated and unpredictable place for businesses. The case for managed services is now stronger than ever. Most anti-virus software uses signatures to detect viruses. This means that every e-mail and website request is scanned to see if anything matches a list of known threats. However, signatures have a weakness. A virus or trojan has to be caught and analysed before the signatures can be updated. This leaves [systems relying upon] them vulnerable to custom-written or brand new threats. With so many new threats emerging around the world, isn't it better to be certain?

14

The Economic Downturn Increases Internet Crime

Karin Brulliard

Karin Brulliard is the Southern Africa correspondent of the Washington Post. Before moving to Johannesburg in 2003, she covered immigration for the newspaper's metro desk and spent two months in Baghdad for the foreign desk.

America has endured one of the worst recessions in its history, with millions losing retirement funds, homes, and jobs. Nigerian scammers have found that the hard economic times have boosted their "trade," however. People more readily believe in fantastic fortunes or outlandish lottery wins, and scammers make tens of thousands of dollars a month. With a mixture of high-tech and voodoo, scammers prey on those who hope against reason and better knowledge.

Online swindling takes dedication even in the best of times, the scammer said earnestly.

The spinal cord aches from sitting at a desk. The eyes itch from staring at a computer. The heart thumps from drinking bitter cola to stay awake for chats with Americans in faraway time zones. The wallet shrinks from buying potions that supposedly compel the Americans to pay.

Working Hard to Defraud Americans

Succeeding in the midst of a worldwide economic meltdown? That, he said, takes even firmer resolve.

"We are working harder. The financial crisis is not making it easy for them over there," said Banjo, 24, speaking about Americans, whose trust he has won and whose money he has fleeced, via his Dell laptop. "They don't have money. And the money they don't have, we want."

Now financially squeezed, Americans succumb even more easily to offers of riches, experts say.

Banjo is a polite young man in a button-down shirt, and he is the sort of guy on the other end of that block-lettered missive requesting your "URGENT ASSISTANCE" in transferring millions of dollars. He is the sort who made Nigeria infamous for cyberscams, which experts say are increasing in these tough times.

U.S. authorities say Americans—the easiest prey, according to Nigerian scammers—lose hundreds of millions of dollars a year to cybercrimes, including a scheme known as the Nigerian 419 fraud, named for a section of the Nigerian criminal code. Now financially squeezed, Americans succumb even more easily to offers of riches, experts say.

Though statistics are fuzzy, the FBI [Federal Bureau of Investigation]-backed Internet Crime Complaint Center says that scam reports by Americans grew 33 percent last year [2008], and that after the United States and Britain, Nigeria housed the most perpetrators. Ultrascan, a Dutch research firm that investigates complaints of 419 fraud, says online scam offers from Nigerians in and outside their homeland have mushroomed this year.

Heroes of Underground Scammers

Nigerian officials dispute their country's prominence in online fraud, noting that scam networks rely on agents around the globe. But 419 is cemented in Nigerian popular culture. The scammers, known as "yahoo-yahoo boys," are glorified in pop songs such as "Yahoozee," which gained even more fame after former secretary of state Colin L. Powell danced to it at a London festival last year.

"My maga don pay/Shout alleluia!" goes another Nigerian anthem, which celebrates, in slang and pidgin English, that a victim—maga—sent money.

Wireless Internet has allowed scammers to move from cybercafes into private residences to churn out e-mails. Nigerian scammers are mostly young men who learn from one another, often as apprentices of cartel-like schemes.

"I'm selling greed," said Felix, 29, an e-mail swindler. "You didn't apply for any lotto, and all of a sudden you just see a mail in your mailbox that you're going to win money? That means you have to be greedy."

Some e-mails promise wealth, perhaps in the form of jewels trapped in the bank box of a deceased dictator, but later require victims to wire "fees" for paperwork or insurance. Dating scams promise love, but eventually the sweetheart needs cash. The most sophisticated lure investors to view venture opportunities in foreign lands—and persuade them, over fake business meetings, to sink millions.

In good months he has made $30,000, which he blew on clothes, hotel rooms and Dom Perignon at "VVIP" clubs.

Felix, like four other self-proclaimed scammers interviewed, did not want his full name published for fear of arrest or angering allies. But the swindlers spoke as if conning were an ordinary trade—one made more cutthroat in challenging times.

An Ordinary Trade

Felix and Banjo said they started as college students. Their campus, one state away from Lagos, teemed with young men with fancy cars, designer clothing and beautiful girlfriends—scammers all.

In the lingo of swindlers, Felix said he went "on the street." He got "tools": formats, or "FMs," for letters; "mailers," or accounts that send e-mails in bulk; and huge lists of e-mail addresses, bought online.

In good months, he said, he has made $30,000, which he blew on clothes, hotel rooms and Dom Perignon at "VVIP" clubs. These days, he lamented, proceeds are down 40 percent.

Chidi Nnamdi Igwe, a professor at the University of Regina in Canada, said jobless young Nigerians got the idea in the 1970s from news reports about corrupt politicians funneling oil proceeds to foreign bank accounts. Scammers began posting letters in the 1980s and later moved to e-mail, said Igwe, author of *Taking Back Nigeria From 419*.

Nigerian authorities insist they are tough on 419 perpetrators. The Economic and Financial Crimes Commission says the cases made up 45 percent of its prosecutions from 2003 to 2006. Commission spokesman Femi Babafemi said authorities nab scammers in frequent cybercafe raids. The commission also is adopting software that sifts through e-mails sent from Nigeria to block scams, he said.

"These things are giving Nigeria a bad image," said Babafemi, adding that scammers' overseas partners and victims lured by promises of wealth should share blame.

Selling Greed

Frank Engelsman, an Ultrascan researcher, said curbing e-mail scams requires better cross-border cooperation among law enforcement. Others say public awareness is the key. But online victim support groups abound. U.S. embassy, bank and money-transfer-agency Web sites display warnings about scams.

Still, people get duped.

"My fiancee is there in Lagos. . . . She is an American . . . she speaks with a heavy African accent after being there for two years," one smitten American wrote to the U.S. Consulate in Lagos, pleading for help. "I have attempted to send her money so that she can leave the country, and both times the guy at Western Union stole the money."

Banjo said his most lucrative swindle is the work-from-home scam, which authorities warn is flourishing as the world sheds jobs. In U.S. newspapers and on the Web, he places ads for "pickup agents" or "correspondents." They print out counterfeit corporate checks—Honeywell is one company whose checks Banjo said he faked—at $10 apiece and mail them to other unsuspecting folks.

Banjo said he has traveled six hours to the forest, where a magician sells scam-boosters.

Those victims then cash the checks and wire the funds to the scammer's accomplice in Britain or South Africa—places less likely to elicit the sender's suspicion. After taking a cut, that person wires the rest to Banjo. Days later, when the bank deems the check phony, the casher must pay.

In good months, Banjo said, he has made $60,000.

But in these tough times, the scammers said, they are relying more on a crucial tool: voodoo. At times, Banjo said, he has traveled six hours to the forest, where a magician sells scam-boosters. A $300 powder supposedly helps scammers "speak with authority" when demanding payment. A powder, rubbed on the face, reportedly makes victims viewing the scammer through webcams powerless to say no.

Relying on Magic for Success

"No matter what, they will pay," said Olumide, a college student, adding that he is boosting his romance scams by wearing a magical, live tortoise hanging from a cord around his neck.

Sometimes, Banjo said, he has so pitied victims that he returned their money. There was Katrina, in Cleveland, who wanted to go to after-Christmas sales. And there was Jimmy.

"Jimmy, Jimmy, Jimmy," Banjo said over a Red Bull, straining to remember. "Somewhere in Florida? Florida. Yes, Florida."

Jimmy was a truck driver. Banjo was Monica, the American owner of a boutique in Nigeria. The boutique burned down, and Jimmy wired money. Jimmy sent money for Monica's flights to the United States, which she missed three times. Jimmy broke it off after dispatching a total of $25,000, Banjo said, but could not stay away.

"He was still asking, 'Just come home. Just come home, baby,'" Banjo recalled.

Banjo said he wired $1,000 to Jimmy and told him that he had been duped.

"There is another thing scammers always say in Nigeria," Banjo said, "that every day, another maga is born in America."

15

Youtube Boosts Rogue Internet Pharmacies

Kristina Peterson, Jacob Pearson, Vytenis Didziulis, and Danielle Douglas

Kristina Peterson, Jacob Pearson, Vytenis Didziulis, and Danielle Douglas were members of the Stabile Investigative Reporting Class of 2009 at the Graduate School of Journalism, Columbia University.

Unlawful pharmacies are increasingly invading YouTube with video ads. And although the site does not profit directly from sales, it does little to counteract the spread of videos promoting cheap Viagra, Cialis, or Prozac. The dangers for consumers are considerable, as they might pay for products that will never arrive or pills of unclear origin and effect. While police are starting to investigate cyber-crimes, however, YouTube is not breaking any laws and the Internet business of selling cheap medications is thriving.

A young man wearing a white polo shirt, glasses and a baseball cap faces the camera. For a few moments his lips move before the video's sound kicks in.

"I just bought some Valium and Xanax from this online pharmacy," Bijan814 says in a YouTube video of roughly 10 seconds. Posted next to his video, a box directs viewers to the Web site *anti-anxiety-pills.com*, where they can buy drugs without a prescription.

While Internet pharmacies are nothing new, some of their promoters have begun to log onto YouTube to post videos such as these, publicizing Web sites that allow customers to purchase drugs online without a prescription.

Over the past four months, students at Columbia University's Stabile Center for Investigative Journalism have researched this development, starting with a focused search using the query terms "buy online" and a list of controlled substances from the Food and Drug Administration. We found close to 170 such videos that have nearly 65,000 hits. And then we went online and bought generic Prozac from one of the promoted sites—without ever having a prescription.

A Blooming Business

Most of these YouTube videos are rough and cheaply produced. In one, a camera slowly pans around a sealed bottle of the stimulant Adderall before zeroing in on a cascade of pills poured on top of a laptop computer. "Buy Adderall online now from our new online store: click the link in the top right hand corner to buy now," says a pop-up box at the screen's base. At one point last month the clip had pulled in nearly 5,000 viewings.

In October [2008], Congress passed the Ryan Haight Act, which explicitly prohibits the online sale of controlled drugs in the U.S. without at least one in-person doctor visit, building on earlier legislation that regulates controlled substances. Still, most of these videos lead viewers to at least 15 Web sites that allow them to order drugs online without a valid prescription.

"We do not require prescriptions but we recommend that they speak to their doctor before taking the medicine," said Tony Walker, a customer service representative for *anti-anxiety-pills.com*.

We asked John Horton, president of an online pharmacy verification site, *LegitScript.com*, to examine these 15 sites.

"There's no question about it; these sites are operating unlawfully and are dangerous," he said.

But there's little incentive for YouTube to take down these traffic-driving videos. Many of the search pages that display these videos contain paid advertisements. And these ads generate revenue for YouTube, which is owned by Google.

YouTube videos that promote online pharmacies are not hard to find.

Google Shrugs Off Monitoring

YouTube videos that promote online pharmacies are not hard to find. Just type in "oxycodone" and "buy online," as we did, and links to numerous videos pop up. After our investigation unearthed 170 videos for various prescription-only drugs, we decided to test one out. We logged on to *n1pills.com*, a Web site promoted by many of those videos, and ordered 30 pills of generic Prozac for $37.97 plus $10.95 in shipping. All we had to do was fill out a short medical questionnaire—we never spoke to a doctor. Just over two weeks later, the drugs—plus two Viagra tablets thrown in for free—arrived, wrapped in a sheet of the *Bombay Times*.

The pills were sent from Pratham Pharma, Shop No. 8 in Mumbai and were labeled a "sample for trade" and "without commercial value," according to the customs slip. Multiple requests to n1pills for comment were not returned.

So we contacted Google to see if they were concerned—both about the number of these videos and their content.

We emailed a link for one suspicious video to Scott Rubin, a Google spokesperson who answers questions on behalf of YouTube. Almost immediately, YouTube pulled it. Rubin said the video was taken down due to a violation of the community guidelines. Those standards prohibit users from posting unsuitable videos that YouTube says break its "common sense rules." He said YouTube could not be expected to monitor every posted clip, with 15 hours of video uploaded on the site every minute. Instead, he said, YouTube defers to their "hundreds of millions" of viewers to flag videos they think violate the guidelines. "We have a system to take down any video that violates the guidelines, whether there are others like it or it is a singular violation," he said.

Similar videos will remain unless users point them out. Rubin said there is no specific threshold number at which point YouTube on its own would take down all impermissible videos.

Online Pharmacies Generate Revenue

And based on its business model, which relies on traffic generated by videos, YouTube can earn revenue from the postings. After Google, YouTube is the second most popular search engine. When a user searches on YouTube, a list of related ads appear on screen. These "sponsored links" come from advertisers, who pay every time users click on their ads.

Last year [2008] Google made just over $21 billion in total advertising revenue, according to its 2008 annual report. Sites that use Google to advertise, including YouTube, account for 31 percent of Google's ad revenue, according to the annual report. But YouTube by itself is not profitable; analysts at Credit Suisse predict the site will lose $470 million in 2009.

YouTube does not accept ads for drugs sold online, Rubin said. So we showed him numerous sponsored links to online pharmacies and asked him to explain why these were on YouTube search pages.

Rubin said that those ads were sold through Google, which allows online pharma ads. Internet drugstores can advertise on Google network sites so long as they are approved by *PharmacyChecker.com*, an independent company that vets online pharmacies and affiliate sites that link to them.

But we found that this system is not exactly foolproof. One YouTube paid ad—not a video—directs viewers to *Oxy codone.Wholesalevipclub.com*. But that site would never be verified by Pharmacy Checker, said its vice president, Gabriel Levitt. "We've never had a member that had 'oxycodone' in its name," he said.

When we tried to purchase oxycodone, the site charged us $29.95 for a membership and forwarded us to a page that listed oxycodone as "in stock."

Then, just a couple of days later, the link on the ad was changed to *Cheapmeds.wholesalevipclub.com*. Experts said Web sites sometimes tweak their sub-domain names to circumvent verification standards. In this case, the site swapped "oxycodone" with "cheapmeds." As of today, *Oxycodone.wholesale vipclub.com* is once again advertising on YouTube.

Bending the Rules

"Sometimes they do it to obfuscate the rules," said John Horton, president of online pharmacy verification site, *LegitScript .com*. Cheapmeds did not answer multiple questions sent via email, but did confirm that they offer oxycodone.

"Yes we sell oxycodone," said someone responding from a customer service email account. "If you join [the membership site] and need help finding it please email for assistance."

Despite appearances, the site does not actually sell drugs—it just refers users to other sites that do, Levitt said. When we tried to purchase oxycodone, the site charged us $29.95 for a membership and forwarded us to a page that listed oxycodone as "in stock." But when we tried to buy the drugs, the site shuttled us back to the same membership page asking for another $29.95.

When we asked about Cheapmeds, Pharmacy Checker terminated the site's membership that day. Levitt would not say why, but reiterated that Cheapmeds was simply a referral site. Still, the paid link was never pulled from YouTube and several days later its membership had been reinstated.

Rubin said Google has faith in Pharmacy Checker's process. "When a site loses its verification status from Pharmacy-Checker, Google is notified and we take prompt and appropriate action to disable ads from that advertiser until such time as the verification status is reinstated," he said.

And Cheapmeds is not the only example—several other Pharmacy Checker-approved sites have recently had their membership revoked. Levitt said Pharmacy Checker does find through its monitoring that a "small minority" of sites are no longer in compliance. "From time to time, Web sites will act in bad faith," Levitt said. "That's not the norm, but it does happen."

Attracting a Younger Audience

Posting videos on YouTube gives drug salesmen access to a large audience—and a young one.

YouTube estimates most of its users are between 18 and 55, but research shows its audience is significantly younger. Roughly 22 percent of YouTube's viewers are 17 years old or younger, according to February 2009 demographics from comScore, Inc., a company that tracks online behavior.

These users visit the site frequently. Around 51 percent of its users visit the site at least weekly and another 52 percent of visitors between the ages of 18 and 34 share videos often, according to a YouTube fact sheet.

These demographics are important considering that research has found younger children to be susceptible to drug addiction. Almost 9 percent of teenagers between 12 and 17 years old admitted to abusing prescription drugs sometime in the past year, according to a 2006 survey conducted by Columbia University's National Center on Addiction and Substance Abuse.

CASA, a leading research institution on the Internet pharma industry, found that the Internet provides "widespread availability" to prescription drugs. In 2008, it found 365 Web sites either advertising [or] selling prescription drugs, only two of which were legitimate online pharmacies certified by the National Association of Boards of Pharmacy. The number of rogue pharmacies is likely much higher, according to Horton. Legit Script counts 36,438 online pharmacies in its database, of which 234 meet its standards.

A danger is that armed with nothing more than a credit card, children claiming to be at least 18 may be able to purchase drugs online without consulting their parents or visiting a doctor. Many sites only ask customers to fill out an online medical questionnaire.

Two of the sites with the highest number of videos on YouTube direct viewers to a rainbow-colored, easily navigable site offering a broad menu of drugs.

"A legitimate doctor-patient relationship includes a face-to-face consultation," said Joseph Rannazzisi, deputy chief of enforcement for the Drug Enforcement Administration, in a July 2008 report. "Filling out a questionnaire, no matter how detailed, is no substitute for this relationship."

Some of the Web sites that sell drugs insist their customers present valid prescriptions and simply make buying drugs more convenient. But most YouTube videos promote sites that verification agencies never approved.

Two of the sites with the highest number of videos on YouTube, *n1pills.com* and *all4pills.com*, direct viewers to *Ypills.com*, a rainbow-colored, easily navigable site offering a broad menu of drugs. The National Association of Boards of Pharmacies, which vets and inspects online pharmacies, does not list Ypills as a site that passes its standards.

Legitscript.com, the online pharmacy verification site, lists Ypills as a "rogue pharmacy" that is "affiliated with" the GlavMed or "Canadian Pharmacy" network of online drugstores. Legitscript describes GlavMed as "a notorious spamming and counterfeit prescription drug operation" that operates thousands of Web sites from China, Russia and other places.

"GlavMed is believed to have ties to the criminal 'Russian Business Network,'" researchers at Cisco and IronPort said in a 2008 report on Internet threats.

There are some 130 YouTube videos that lead viewers to Ypills, most of them drab slideshows that provide little information other than the Web site's address.

Policing the Internet

YouTube is not breaking any laws. And it is unlikely to be held liable for hosting any of these videos or ads, said experts like Harvard Professor John Palfrey. The Communications Decency Act of 1996 gives Web sites broad free speech protections.

Still, efforts to police Internet activity may be on the rise.

Craig Butterworth, spokesman for the National White Collar Crime Center, said rising numbers of law enforcement agencies are starting cyber crime units and patrolling online activities. "As Internet-based crime continues to proliferate, law enforcement is paying more and more attention," he said.

Some agencies are themselves using YouTube as a means to broadcast their own safety messages. In a June 2007 video, the Food and Drug Administration warns viewers of the hazards of buying drugs online. In between blurry images of a person Googling and extreme close-ups of illegal pills, a spokeswoman sternly advises watchers not to order drugs from illegitimate Web sites.

"Many people are choosing to buy prescription drugs online," the spokeswoman says. "But unless they're very careful, this can be a risky undertaking."

16

Organized Crime Is Taking over the Internet

Oscar McLaren

Oscar McLaren is an Australian journalist.

Organized crime is invading the Internet via botnets—groups of private computers that have been infected by viruses and malware. In fact, criminal activity is threatening to overwhelm online security systems and create a global calamity and safety risk for consumers. The Internet as we know it today might not be sustainable in the future; without a serious discussion about how online users and their computers can be protected, organized crime will hijack the Web and plunge the online community into chaos.

One of Australia's leading figures in online law enforcement says the internet offers so many opportunities for crime that he expects "at some stage there will be real debate on the benefit of the internet."

This has led Detective Superintendent Brian Hay of the Queensland Police Service to suggest that some people might ask: Should we turn it off?

As far as major infrastructure projects go, it does not get much bigger than the National Broadband Network announced by Kevin Rudd earlier this year to "pull Australia out of the broadband dark ages."

But the plan has frayed the nerves of the already overstretched agencies and companies charged with keeping the internet safe.

Oscar McLaren, "Internet Security: Fear in the Fast Lane," *ABC News Australia*, August 17, 2009, http://www.abc.net.au/news/stories/2009/08/17/2657529.htm (August 25, 2009).

For them, the digital future looks dark, and the faster the internet, the darker it could get.

The Threat of Organised Crime

Organised crime is emerging as the biggest threat online, and perhaps most alarming is the role that home computers play in international crime networks.

The criminal gangs' weapons of choice are referred to as botnets—groups of computers that have been infected by small computer programs called malware.

It is estimated that one in every six computers in Australia has at some stage been infected by malware—you can be infected just by opening a suspicious email or even visiting a trusted site that has been secretly hacked.

Some of the best-known sites in Australia have been hacked in this way, including the Sydney Opera House's site.

Once your computer has been infected and becomes part of a botnet, it is under the control of an online criminal who can use it to do just about anything—send spam emails by the thousands or steal your bank account information.

Since 2002, a cyber-crime industry worth hundreds of millions of dollars has flourished, and home computer users have helped out every step of the way.

The largest known botnet has as many as 2 million computers connected to it at any one time and has affected 28 million machines over its lifetime.

Catastrophic Consequences

In 2007, the entire Baltic nation of Estonia was taken offline by a Distributed Denial of Service (DDoS) attack—where the computers in a botnet are instructed to flood a particular site with traffic.

Just last week [in August 2009], the microblogging site Twitter was down for hours at a time because of a DDoS.

With the size of today's botnets, Graham Ingram, the head of Australia's national internet security body AusCERT [Computer Emergency Response Team], worries that a major Western country could be next.

"I believe that it's possible," he said. "The botnets are getting bigger and they are getting more sophisticated and getting more difficult for us to mitigate against."

Credit card and banking details are being sold openly in online forums for a few dollars each.

The financial system is also at risk. It is now so easy to steal credit card and banking details that they are being sold openly in online forums for a few dollars each.

Four Corners [an investigative television program] has been given a guided tour of one such site, which has up to 14,000 people logged onto it at any one time.

Up for sale were stolen credit card details (sold in bulk or individually), fake passports, spam campaigns (priced per million emails) and even entire botnets—priced per thousand computers.

Internet Crime Is Big Business

Police around the country are under no illusions about the scale of the challenge, and Detective Superintendent [Det Supt] Hay gives credit to the criminals where it is due.

"It is a wonderful business model," he said. "It's highly successful. It's self-regulated. It's for all intents and purposes ultimately professional."

The success of the model, and the difficulties of prosecuting international crimes, have forced what Det Supt Hay refers to as "a real paradigm shift."

"Is it more important to lock up one offender or to prevent it from happening to thousands of people?" he said.

"We realise that putting resources, energies and efforts into attempting to prosecute someone overseas is probably not the wisest use of the taxpayer's dollar."

The Australian Federal Police had a recent success when they covertly took control of a criminal online marketplace that was being run from Australia.

They raided at least two Australian-based members of the site, but eventually decided that disruption was the best plan of attack.

Last Thursday [August 13, 2009] officers posted an announcement on the site, informing members that it was under police control and that they should expect a knock at the door.

But as the police have acknowledged, most cyber-criminals are members of multiple sites, and the roaring trade will undoubtedly continue elsewhere.

The question of how else to deal with online crime is not easily answered. A common refrain from police forces is that public education is the key.

There is no serious argument being made that the Internet should be switched off.

Det Supt Hay proffers the mantra of "delete, delete, delete" for any unsolicited email.

"If everyone followed those three simple rules, that would reduce the chances of them falling victim online possibly as much as 80 per cent," he said.

Internet Safety Is Hard to Achieve

But Mr Ingram says computer security is becoming so complicated that education alone is not enough.

He points out that 80 per cent of malware infections come not from email attachments, but from simply visiting trusted sites associated with major institutions and entertainment organisations.

"If we tell people, 'don't click on links in emails that you don't know who they're from' ... that's a really good public approach," he said.

"But if I tell you now that you're not to click on links on the internet, it sort of makes the internet a bit redundant doesn't it?"

At this stage, there is no serious argument being made that the internet should be switched off.

But the fact that it is being raised at all in internet security circles shows how large the problem has become.

The number of malware strains on the internet has nearly doubled in the past year, to 22 million.

The more sophisticated botnets are almost impossible to trace and have self-defence mechanisms that identify and attack anyone who tries to investigate how they work.

Police forces and security companies are under constant attack from hackers around the world.

In their more subdued moments, some experts who spoke to *Four Corners* said simply that they "don't know what the solution is."

But as internet speeds get faster in Australia, computers will become more valuable to online criminals, botnets will become more potent and threats will become more pronounced.

Without a serious debate about internet security, Australia could well go from one dark age to another.

Organizations to Contact

The editors have compiled the following list of organizations concerned with the issues debated in this book. The descriptions are derived from materials provided by the organizations. All have publications or information available for interested readers. The list was compiled on the date of publication of the present volume; the information provided here may change. Be aware that many organizations take several weeks or longer to respond to inquiries, so allow as much time as possible.

Alliance Against Fraud (AAF)
National Consumers League, Washington, DC   20006
(202) 835-3323 • Fax: (202) 835-0747
E-mail: info@nclnet.org
Web site: www.fraud.org/aaft/aaftinfo.htm

The AAF, coordinated by the National Consumers League, is a coalition of public interest groups, trade associations, labor unions, businesses, law enforcement agencies, educators, and consumer protection agencies. AAF members promote efforts to educate the public about telemarketing and Internet fraud and how to shop safely by phone and online. Tips and resources are available on the AAF Web site.

American Council on Consumer Interests (ACCI)
555 E Wells Street # 1100, Milwaukee, WI   53202
(414) 276-6445 • Fax: (414) 276-3349
E-mail: info@consumerinterests.org
Web site: www.consumerinterests.org

ACCI is the leading consumer policy research and education organization consisting of a worldwide community of researchers, educators, and related professionals. The ACCI publishes newsletters, e-news, and its annual report online.

Better Business Bureau (BBB)
4200 Wilson Blvd., Suite 800, Arlington, VA   22203-1838
(703) 276-0100 • Fax: (703) 525-8277
Web site: www.bbb.org

The BBB seeks to establish integrity and performance in the marketplace. Integrity includes respect and ethics; performance speaks to a business's track record of delivering results in accordance with BBB standards and/or addressing customer concerns in a timely, satisfactory manner. The BBB offers guidance to help spot schemes and scams. It also suggests ways to identify whether a company is legitimate or not. Articles on these topics are made available online.

Consumers Union (CU)
101 Truman Ave., Yonkers, NY   10703-1057
(914) 378-2000 • Fax: (914) 378-2900
Web site: www.consumersunion.org

Consumers Union, publisher of *Consumer Reports*, is an independent, nonprofit testing and information organization serving only consumers. It offers advice about products and services, personal finance, health and nutrition, and other consumer concerns. CU posts articles on telemarketing and Internet fraud on its extensive Web site.

Federal Trade Commission (FTC)
600 Pennsylvania Ave. NW, Washington, DC   20580
(202) 326-2222
Web site: www.ftc.gov

The FTC deals with issues of everyday economic life. It is the only federal agency with both consumer protection and competition jurisdiction. The FTC strives to enforce laws and regulations and to advance consumers' interests by sharing its expertise with federal and state legislatures and U.S. and international government agencies. Publications such as *What Is Phishing?* and *Take Charge: Fighting Back Against Identity Theft* can be downloaded from its Web site.

GetNetWise
E-mail: cmatsuda@neted.org
Web site: www.getnetwise.org

GetNetWise is a public service provided by Internet industry corporations and public interest organizations to help Internet users experience safe online research and entertainment. The GetNetWise coalition wants users to make informed decisions about their and their family's use of the Internet. The organization provides articles on spam and kids' safety on its Web site.

Institute for Responsible Online and Cell-Phone Communication (I.R.O.C.²)
PO Box 1131, Mount Laurel, NJ   08054-9998
(877) 295-2005
Web site: www.iroc2.org

I.R.O.C.² is a nonprofit organization advocating digital responsibility, safety, and awareness. It endorses the development and safe use of all digital devices (e.g., digital cameras, cell phones, computers, Internet, video cams, Web cameras, etc.) and the World Wide Web. The organization's creation is based on the fact that many individuals are not aware of the short- and long-term consequences of their own actions when utilizing digital technologies. Articles on sex casting and sexting are available on the organization's Web site.

National Center for Missing & Exploited Children (NCMEC)
Charles B. Wang International Children's Building
Alexandria, VA   22314-3175
(703) 224-2150 • Fax: (703) 224-2122
Web site: www.ncmec.org

The NCMEC's mission is to help prevent child abduction and sexual exploitation. The organization assists in finding missing children and supports victims of child abduction and sexual exploitation. Its Web site provides articles on sexual exploitation, sex offenders, and how to guard against online predators.

OnGuard Online
E-mail: OnGuardOnline@ftc.gov
Web site: www.onguardonline.gov

OnGuardOnline provides tips from the federal government and the technology industry to help consumers be on guard against Internet fraud, to secure computers, and to protect personal information. The Web site offers information and games to test individuals' cyber savviness.

The SANS Institute
8120 Woodmont Ave., Suite 205, Bethesda, MD   20814
(301) 654-SANS (7267) • Fax: (301) 951-0140
E-mail: info@sans.org
Web site: www.sans.org

The SANS (SysAdmin, Audit, Network, Security) Institute was established in 1989 as a research and education organization. Security professionals, auditors, system administrators, and network administrators share the lessons they are learning and jointly find solutions to the challenges they face. The institute also develops, maintains, and makes available at no cost the largest collection of research documents about many aspects of information security.

U.S. Department of Justice, Criminal Division, Computer Crime and Intellectual Property Section (CCIPS)
10th & Constitution Ave. NW, Washington, DC   20530
(202) 514-1026 • Fax: (202) 514-6113
Web site: www.cybercrime.gov

The CCIPS is responsible for implementing the Justice Department's national strategies in combating computer and intellectual property crimes. CCIPS prevents, investigates, and prosecutes computer crimes by working with other government agencies, the private sector, academic institutions, and foreign counterparts. Press releases and brochures on cybercrime, such as the *Prosecuting Computer Crimes Manual*, are accessible through the Web site.

U.S. Public Interest Research Group (U.S. PIRG)
218 D Street SE, Washington, DC   20003-1900
(202) 546-9707 • Fax: (202) 546-2461
E-mail: uspirg@pirg.org
Web site: www.uspirg.org

U.S. PIRG is the national lobbying office for the state public
interest research groups. The PIRGs are consumer and envi-
ronmental advocacy groups that address issues such as bank
fees, identity theft, credit bureau abuses, clean air and clean
water, right to know, campaign finance reform, and various
other issues. U.S. PIRG does not handle individual consumer
complaints directly, but measures complaint levels to gauge
the need for remedial legislation. Newsletters and annual reports are available on its Web site, as is a consumers' blog.

Bibliography

Books

Yaman Akdeniz
Internet Child Pornography and the Law: National and International Responses. Farnham, UK: Ashgate, 2008.

Sharlene Azam
Oral Sex Is the New Goodnight Kiss: The Sexual Bullying of Girls. Bollywood Filmed Entertainment, 2009.

Jack Balkin et al., eds.
Cybercrime: Digital Cops in a Networked Environment. New York: New York University Press, 2006.

Martin Biegelman
Identity Theft Handbook: Detection, Prevention, and Security. Hoboken, NJ: Wiley, 2009.

Susan Brenner
Law in an Era of Smart Technology. Oxford: Oxford University Press, 2007.

John Bush, ed.
Child Safety: From Sexual Predators. CreateSpace, 2008.

Marcus Erooga and Helen Masson, eds.
Children and Young People Who Sexually Abuse Others: Challenges and Responses. London: Routledge, 2006.

Stefan Fafinski
Computer Misuse: Response, Regulation and the Law. Cullompton, England: Willan, 2009.

Peter Grabosky	*Electronic Crime.* New Jersey: Prentice Hall, 2006.
Dennis Howitt and Kerry Sheldon	*Sex Offenders and the Internet.* New York: John Wiley & Sons, 2007.
Yvonne Jewkes, ed.	*Dot.cons: Crime, Deviance, and Identity on the Internet.* Cullompton, England: Willan, 2002.
Samuel McQuade III, James Colt, and Nancy Meyer	*Cyber Bullying: Protecting Kids and Adults from Online Bullies.* New York: Praeger, 2009
Samuel C. McQuade	*Understanding and Managing Cybercrime.* Boston: Allyn & Bacon, 2006.
Scott Mitic	*Stopping Identity Theft: 10 Easy Steps to Security.* Berkeley, CA: NOLO, 2009.
Michael Newton	*The Encyclopedia of High-Tech Crime and Crime-Fighting.* New York: Checkmark Books, 2004.
Jean Rusin	*Poison Pen Pal: Secrets, Lies, and Online Predators.* Bloomington, IN: AuthorHouse, 2006.
David Schwartz	*Cutting the Wire: Gaming Prohibition and the Internet.* Reno, NV: University of Nevada Press, 2005.
Jim Stickley	*The Truth About Identity Theft.* Upper Saddle River, NJ: FT Press, 2008.

Mike Sullivan

Online Predators. Longwood, FL: Xulon Books, 2008.

Max Taylor and Ethel Quayle

Child Pornography: An Internet Crime, New York: Brunner-Routledge, 2003.

Ian Walden

Computer Crimes and Digital Investigations. Oxford: Oxford University Press, 2007.

David Wall

Cybercrimes: The Transformation of Crime in the Information Age. Cambridge, UK: Polity, 2007.

Matthew Williams

Virtually Criminal: Crime, Deviance and Regulation Online. London: Routledge, 2006.

Majid Yar

Cybercrime and Society. London: Sage, 2006.

Periodicals

Yaman Akdeniz

"Governing Racist Content on the Internet: National and International Responses," *University of New Brunswick Law Journal* (Canada), Spring 2007.

Stuart Allison, Amie Schuck, and Kim Lersch

"Exploring the Crime of Identity Theft: Prevalence, Clearance Rates, and Victim/Offender Characteristics," *Journal of Criminal Justice,* volume 33, no. 1. January-February 2005.

Carolyn Bigda

"ID Theft: Are You the Next Victim?" *Money,* May 1, 2006.

Bruce Bower	"Internet Seduction: Online Sex Offenders Prey on At-Risk Teens," *Science News*, February 23, 2008.
Bruce Bower	"Growing up Online: Young People Jump Headfirst into the Internet's World," *Science News*, June 17, 2006.
Susan Brenner	"U.S. Cybercrime Law: Defining Offenses," *Information Systems Frontiers*, 2004.
Curriculum Review	"Teens Share Sexually Explicit Messages: Simple Rebellion or Dangerous Behavior?" May 2009.
Kristin Davis	"Can You Smell the Phish?" *Kiplinger's Personal Finance*, February 2005.
The Economist	"If in Doubt, Farm It Out," June 1, 2006.
Federal Trade Commission	"Statement of the Federal Trade Commission Before the Committee on Commerce, Science, and Transportation, U.S. Senate, on Data Breaches and Identity Theft," June 16, 2005.
Lee Gomes	"Phisher Tales: How Webs of Scammers Pull off Internet Fraud," *The Wall Street Journal*, June 20, 2005.
Kevin Jepson	"Giving the Thumb to Fraud," *Credit Union Journal*, 2005.

Yvonne Jewkes and Carol Andrews
"Policing the Filth: The Problems of Investigating Online Child Pornography in England and Wales," *Policing and Society*, vol. 15, no. 1. March 2005.

Monica Jones
"Your Child and the Internet: Tips to Keep Them Safe on the Information Superhighway," *Ebony*, March 2006.

Jason Krause
"Stolen Lives," *ABA Journal*, March 2006.

Thomas Leary
"Identity Theft and Social Security Numbers," *Electronic Banking Law and Commerce Report*, 2005.

Maureen Macfarlane
"Misbehavior in Cyberspace: The Rise in Social Networking Sites and Chat Rooms Intermingles Free Expression and Student Safety in Cyberspace," *School Administrator*, October 2007.

Karl Menninger
"Identity Theft and Other Misuses of Credit and Debit Cards," *American Jurisprudence Proof of Facts*, 2005.

Benjamin Radford
"Predator Panic: A Closer Look," *Skeptical Inquirer*, September 2006.

Paul Rodriguez
"Virtual Child Porn's Very Real Consequences," *Insight on the News*, May 27, 2002.

State Legislatures
"The Vexing Issue of 'Sexting,'" July 2009.

Washington Times   "School Districts Hope Students Get the Picture About 'Sexting' Dangers," July 23, 2009.

Perry A. Zirkel   "All a Twitter About Sexting: Sexual Content in Text Messages Raises Legal Questions for Schools," *Phi Delta Kappan*, October 1, 2009.

Index

N

N1pills.com, 83, 86

National Association of Boards of Pharmacy, 86

National Broadband Network (Australia), 89

National Campaign to Prevent Teen and Unplanned Pregnancy, 47, 48

National Center for Missing and Exploited Children, 19, 22

National Center on Addiction and Substance Abuse of Columbia University, 85

National Consumers League (NCL), 54–55

National Cyber Security Alliance, 56

National Fraud Information Center of NCL, 55

National Organization of Women, 33

Native American casinos, 44

NBA (National Basketball Association), 36

NCAA (National Collegiate Athletic Association), 36

Netflix, 27

New York Times, 21, 24

NFL (National Football League), 36

NHL (National Hockey League), 36

Nielsen survey, 31

Nigerian 419 fraud, 75

O

O'Brien, Thomas, 64

Ogilvie, Alan, 8

Ohio, 35, 46

Ohio State University, 56

Online sexual abuse
    exaggeration, 14–19
    personal story, 20–25
    stranger concept, 8–9
    target age, 11–13
    teenager participation, 9–10

Oregon, 20

Organized crime, 89–93

Oxycodone.Wholesalevipclub.com, 84

P

Palfrey, John, 15, 87

Pandora, 27

Parents, 28

Pearson, Jacob, 80–88

Pedophilia, 8, 46

Peer-to-peer file sharing, 22

Peterson, Kristina, 80–88

Pharmacies online, 80–88

Pharmacy Checker, 84–85

Phishing, 50–56, 69, 70

Physical abuse, 13

Poker, 38–44

Poker Players Alliance, 43

Pornography
    child/adult online communication and, 13
    child pornography, 22–23, 30–34
    fake pornography, 58
    rape and, 31–32
    sexting, 45–49

Powell, Colin L., 76

Powell, Lynn, 46

PR Newswire, 54–56

Project Safe Childhood initiative, 25